# HARBOURS & PORTS



The Cargo Lifeline

SHASHANK SHEKHAR TIWARI

NOTION PRESS

NOTION PRESS

India. Singapore. Malaysia.

ISBN xxx-x-xxxxx-xx-x

# Contents

# Preface

Writing a preface is one of the toughest things a person needs to do, but anyways it has to be written, so let's get done with it.

The idea of this book came into existence only after I started working on a road and bridges project in India. After working for a few months, I asked myself what are the major components of ports, how does each function and what are the ins and outs. From there on I started reading about ports and gather as much information as I could. After a few months of reading, I decided to put everything together in the form of a book for people like me to go through for a beginner's knowledge about ports and its different components.

Ports have always fascinated me ever since I was a child. I loved how easily they are able to handle such Mega size monstrous ships and their humongous size cargo. With all those large number of machineries and equipment's running all around, there never seems to be any issues in any case with the operations or the outputs of the ports.

This book will cover all the components of the port and will explain in detail about each one of them so that people can understand it easily.

So, let's dive into it and discover the world of PORTS and try to understand it from a layman's point of view.

Shashank Shekhar Tiwari

15 September 2021

# Acknowledgments

This book couldn't have been possible if it weren't for my family members who have been a constant support from the very start of this book about a year back.

Whenever a new book comes out a lot a work goes into it by the author, the editors, the publishers and everyone involved with the book in one way or another, to make it easily available and easy reference for people to use and understand, this is one such which has been designed for everyone's easy understanding.

This book on ports is designed in such a way that even if a person with no knowledge on harbours & ports go through this can easily understand different components and parts of ports. It also explains in detail how the different components of port function together and come out as a single entity.

So, without wasting any time further, let's dive right into it and discover the beautiful world of port and shipping industry.

# 1. Introduction

*Past, Present and Future*

Maritime transportation has generally been the most convenient and least expensive means of transporting goods, and in today's world it carries over 80% of the cargo. This is why mankind, since ancient times, has been steadily extending its activities into this area.

The history of maritime transportation and port development dates back to as early as 3700 B.C. Over centuries, transport of goods by means of water transportation has been evolving in steps with the needs of the world trade and the technical capabilities to build larger and more cost-effective ships that can handle cargo facilities.

Initially, traffic on water was only on a local level basis where small ships sailed out of river ports for other nearby river ports located in the same river system. With advancing navigational skills and invention of compass the merchants ventured greater and greater distances without the fear of being lost in the open seas.

Thus, large ships transporting large quantities of goods emerged. As the ship traffic increased and bigger ships came into picture, the existing river ports became overcrowded, and in order to permit more ships of various sizes to berth, and at the same time to keep the river usable for other ships, piers had to be constructed along river banks.

This stage may be seen as the beginning of the development of modern ports. The ever-increasing demand for shipping and port facilities resulted in construction of the first open-sea ports.

Over five thousand years ago the Lothal of the Indus valley civilisation, located in the Bhal region of the modern state of Gujarat established open sea ports along the coastline of Lothal City, and the Romans built the famous naval port near Rome on the Tiber River at Ostia. By the end of the first century A.D. a number of large ports had been constructed in the Mediterranean, the Red Sea, and the Persian Gulf.

Unfortunately, many of these old ports and harbours have disappeared, either being destroyed during the wars, destroyed by the water bodies they were built on, buried by earthquakes, or just through neglect and decadence. Some of these ports are known from old documents and others have been discovered by archaeologists. As pointed out by famous archaeologist, those ports were well planned and effectively executed. The description of different methods of port construction in earlier centuries, specifically during the Roman Empire, that include the use of tongue and grooved, laminated, and various other types of sheet piling, and large stone blocks are found in ancient documents by Roman architects.

As ship navigators developed more skill and fears of unknown waters gradually disappeared, mariners, in addition to trade between river ports on their own coasts, started sailing the high seas, bringing goods from country to country and from continent to continent. The interchange of goods and later of raw materials between countries and continents reached by maritime traffic as well as the development of powerful navy fleets brought about development of large sea ports; this subsequently gave birth to larger cities built around these ports.

Many modern cities have been built and expanded around medieval ports located on the open sea, bays, and rivers. Examples are Varanasi, Delhi, Kolkata, London, Rotterdam, Hamburg, and many others. However, it was not until the mid-19th century that a revival of interest in port works reappeared.

Picture 1.1 New quay wall with lifeboat from late 1890s.

Port developments and their evolution started due to both economic and technological pressures that resulted from the global industrial revolution. At this time, the size, diversity, and complexity of ports changed dramatically. To a great extent this have been influenced by the changing nature of ships. For example, the transition from ships made from wood to steel and the introduction and rapid development of steamboats, and by the demand that greater volumes of cargo be handled at ports more rapidly. The latter triggered the development of more and more efficient methods and technologies for handling and hauling of miscellaneous cargoes. However, in the 19th century many kinds of cargos were still handled manually as it had been for centuries. Cargoes that consisted basically of bags, pieces of timber, steel, bundles, barrels, cases, cartons, drums, and so forth have been moved manually into the ship, on the quay, in the shed, and in the warehouse, sometimes humped on the back. This created a heavy demand for labour which fluctuated greatly with the arrival and departure of ships. Thus, if the ships were to be turned round efficiently and economically, a big pool of casual labourers was necessary.

In the late 19th century, ships still continued their transition from sail to steam engine. The capacity of these vessels was a few thousand tonnes and their draft less than 6 m. As ships changed, so did the ports that served them.

In many ports, the finger pier was the most characteristic type of berth construction. Typically, goods were stored there in warehouses located in close proximity to the berth line and were taken in and out of port by carts. The shift to mechanized handling of cargoes in ports began in the early 1900s. This was largely dictated by the growing volume of maritime traffic and changing size of ships. By the 1920s most of the general cargo ships were using onboard booms to move cargo by the sling-load method. The trend toward the growth of ship size coincided with construction of vessels specialized in transporting a certain type of cargo (e.g., general purpose commodities, dry and liquid bulk cargoes, and others). Naturally, new developments in a ship industry inevitably brought about innovations in cargo handling and hauling technologies, the most radical of which was introduction of a quay edge cranes.

Picture 1.2 Quay edge cranes

Second World War inspired revolutionary ideas took mechanization of cargo handling a step farther by the introduction of forklift trucks and pallets that enabled the general-purpose cargoes to be moved faster. In the years after the great wars, pallets have been standardized internationally by International Standard Organization (ISO-1992). The ISO Committee stipulated that the maximum permissible width of road vehicles (then mostly flat and open) must be about 245 cm; thus, all standard pallets had one dimension, of which 245 cm was a multiple, so that they could be stowed across open vehicles without wasting space. The use of forklift vehicles and pallets was very rapidly developed in industries all over the world, and palletized loads occupied the steadily increasing volume of ship holds. This, however, changed drastically in the not-too-distant future. The shift to new technologies occurred in the 1950s with the introduction of container ships built to transport large freight containers.

Containers were soon standardized by ISO internationally to 20ft/40 ft in length (6.06 m/12.19 m) with the outside width and height being 8 ft (2.44 m). At the present time, the empty weight of a modern 20-ft container weights around 2,300kg with maximum permitted total weight of 25,000kg. The empty weight of a 40-ft container is around 3,750kg with a maximum permitted total weight of 27,600kg.

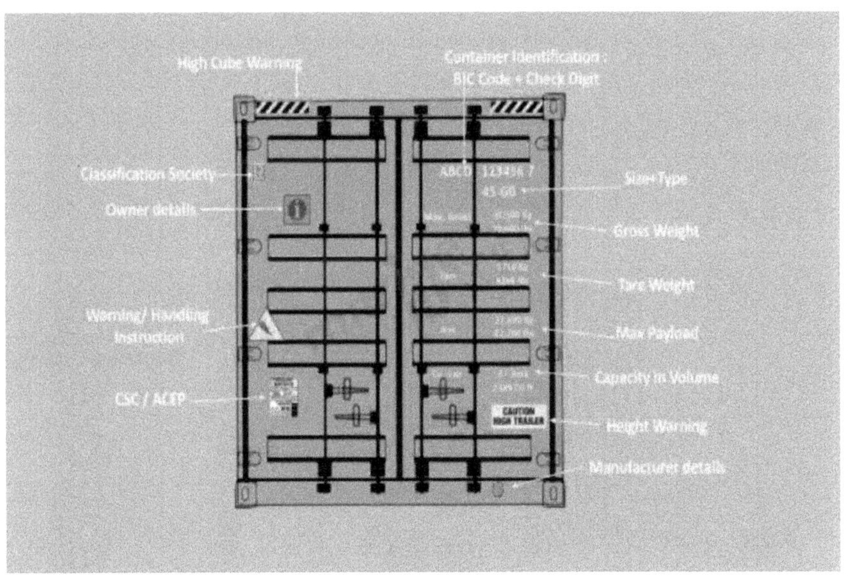


Picture 1.3 Specifications of a shipping container

| 20 ft Container | | | |
|---|---|---|---|
| Dimensions | External | 6.058×2.438×2.591 | M |
| | | 20×8×8.5 | FT |
| | Internal | 5.898×2.350×2.390 | M |
| Door Opening(W*H) | | 2.336×2.280 | M |
| Inside Cubic Capacity | | 33 | CBM |
| Maximum Gross Weight | | 30,480 | KG |
| Tare Weight | | 2,200 | KG |
| Maximum Payload | | 28,280 | KG |

Picture 1.4 Size of a shipping container

Initially, containers have been handled by conventional quay edge cranes. The first specially designed container crane was introduced in 1959, and over the last 30 years, container handling cranes have grown in size and handling capacity. The need for efficient handling of containers stimulated the development of new equipment, such as straddle carriers, heavy lift forklift trucks, gantry cranes, special tractors, and others. Older forklift trucks used for handling general cargo and pallets had lifting capacities of only a few thousand kilograms. In contrast, today's new forklifts for container handling have capacities up to 45,000 kg. During the last 25 years, the roll-on/rolloff method of handling containers have been developed and used extensively. This method allows containers, but also cars, tracks, trains, and so forth, to roll on ships via large stern or side ramps.

Picture 1.5 Heavy forklift trucks

Picture 1.6 a. special tractor, b. Gantry cranes

Picture 1.7 Straddle carriers

Picture 1.8 Roll-on/Roll-off container

The advent of containers completely overshadowed cargo handling on pallets. The introduction of container systems for transporting goods revolutionized sea and land transport and cargo handling methods; ship turnaround time was reduced spectacularly and speed, efficiency, and safety of handling all types of container cargoes increased dramatically. This new technology drastically changed the approach to port planning. In most ports, a previously very effective pier system was disused as general cargo operations have been moved to the usually remote, high-volume container facilities with their large paved container storage areas and relatively few berths.

These modern specialized ports and terminals tie directly into upland staging areas (marshalling yards) with multimodal links to several cities, a region, or the entire country. Traditionally, ports have been developed in natural harbours and, as mentioned earlier, had formed the nuclei for many cities. Today, marine terminals and ports are built wherever they can be economically justified. The need for large open areas to accommodate a modern container facility has induced ports to move to the periphery of cities and often on poor quality land. The latter usually presents a challenge to port designers and has been an area of major controversy related mostly to dredging and disposal of the contaminated dredged soils.

Picture 1.9 Marshalling Yard

Alternatives to dredging have been found in constructing offshore island ports and moving the up-river shallow draft ports down river, to deeper waters. Dramatic changes have also occurred in the handling of liquid and dry bulk cargos. Movements of liquid bulk petroleum products by ship started in the late 19th century when special tanks were mounted onto existing vessels. Prior to this, the only means of moving liquids was in barrels, which was not a very efficient way of transporting ever-increasing quantities as mankind moved into the age of petroleum.

Since the introduction of the first tank mounted vessels, the procedure and method of liquid bulk handling has not changed in principle 100 years later; however, technical improvements in this area have been spectacular. The capacity of liquid bulk carriers (tankers) in the 1940s has reached 22,000 Deadweight tonnage (DWT) and at the present time 550,000 DWT tankers ply the oceans. Today, several shipyards in Europe and Asia have the capacity to build 1,000,000-DWT tankers. Similar developments have occurred in the transportation of dry bulk materials. Bulk carriers have lagged but tracked tanker growth, and, similarly, tankers may also be expected to grow in the future. The use of large and very large deep draft ships for transporting liquid and dry bulk materials and the material hauling innovations have changed the nature of the modern port. Ports actually become a highly specialized terminals able to handle the one specific cargo at very high rates; for example, loading of up to 20,000 tonnes/h and more of dry bulk, and 220,000 m3 of crude oil per day; thus, annual throughput of tens of millions of tonnes has been achieved.

Deep draft vessels need deep water ports. It has been learned, however, that the conventional approach to construction of such ports, involving dredging of large quantities of sometimes contaminated sediments, can be unavoidably very expensive. The solution has been found in the construction of offshore marine facilities not protected from the effects of environmental forces such as waves and currents. At these facilities, the low berth occupancy due to rough sea conditions has been compensated for by a very high rate of material handling on calm days.

These facilities have been constructed far enough offshore where sufficiently deep water is found and no maintenance dredging is needed. In some instances, the terminals have been moved as far as 2 km or more offshore and have been linked to the shore either by a trestle bridge, designed to support pipe lines or conveyor systems and to provide access to the terminal for lightweight vehicular traffic or by submarine pipelines. In some instances, particularly in heavily populated areas where local residents object to the construction of conventional trestles as an unacceptable "visual pollution," submarine tunnels have been constructed as a solution to the problem.

Picture 1.10 Trestle Bridge

The modern port is developed as an important link in a total transportation system and planners of such multimodal systems seek to optimize the total network, not just one of its components. Construction of a new port, or expansion or modernization of an existing one, is usually carried out to increase port capacity and its effectiveness. Traditionally, this has been focused on the sea, and consequently, construction of new berths and modernization and expansion of existing ones was the prime area of interest. However, as urban coastal areas, particularly in developed countries, have substantially expanded over the last five decades, while concurrently international trade has increased and continue to expand, making the world more and more economically interdependent, the port land-side capacity to transfer the cargo from the wharf to the end user has become increasingly critical. In some densely populated areas, the available transportation network (e.g., highway and rail) is limited to moving a certain amount of cargo and cannot be expanded further. Under these conditions there is no logic in increasing the existing port capacity, unless the land-side transportation infrastructure is equally capable of moving the increased volume of cargo through the land-based transportation network.

In this respect, to avoid a waterfront conflict, many countries developed master plans for their major ports. For example, in Canada, both the Canada Ports Corporation (a Canadian Crown Corporation) and individual ports have developed land use plans and economic impact assessment in cooperation with the cities and local special-interest groups which interface with port activities similar is the case with Port Modernization & New Port Development in India. Here also the port authorities along with individual groups and NGT and working together for expansion and modernization of existing ports so that it does not have a negative effect on the surroundings. In the view of many experts, modernization of existing ports will continue and many new ports will be developed in the 2020s and beyond due to major expansion of the world economy. The latter is result of dramatic growth of the world population, general industrial growth, and growth of petroleum and mineral material industries. The real value of world trade will continue to grow. Asia Pacific Trade Agreement APTA and with India's active participation in Global System of Trade Preferences GSTP, will encourage other developing economies of the world to move forward with their port development and modernization. As was the case with The North American Free Trade Agreement (NAFTA) between the United States, Canada, and Mexico and new improved GATT treaty arrangements encouraged many similar agreements elsewhere in the world that eventually resulted in the total world market and free from protectionism and immune to destabilizing political upheaval in some regions.

As per the latest trend we can see that the exporters will seek to increase the added value of their trade, which will tend to reduce tonnages of raw commodities and increase those in partially or fully processed materials (Similar to food products). Thus, increasingly refined petroleum products, chemicals, alumina or aluminium ingots or aluminium products, steel products, vehicles, sawn and processed timber products, processed agricultural commodities and such-like will be the cargoes rather than the basic raw commodities. These are more valuable and readily damaged cargoes which require more careful handling and storage. The trend to more specialized vessels such as reefer, parcel tanker, car carriers and roll-on/roll-off will continue and many of the processed cargoes will end up being handled in containers.

This trend is very clearly visible in Asia (over $6.7 trillion worth of exports were done by Asia alone in 2019, with China amounting to over a third of the total exports in Asia and around 20% of the total world's exports). For example, today, China's exports consist of over 75% manufactured goods as opposed to export of raw materials and this trend is characteristic of most countries in South East Asia. Wider, nonstandard container are already the reality, and the trend for use of larger containers will continue. New container sizes will inevitably have great impact on the design of new containerships and the container handling technologies. The most radical and far-reaching changes in container terminal technology will be their continuing automation which will lower manpower requirements and operating costs, increase control, and speed of the flow of goods through the ports. Future terminals will be more flexible and easily adaptable to changes in the world's economy resulting in cyclic changes in demands.

Alternatives to dredging and construction of deep-water ports will be designed for wider vessels with lesser drafts (Due to the new trend of shipping industry, where the ships operation speed has been reducing drastically to be more economical and use of alternative sources of energy to propel the ships leading to new ship designs which enable them to travel in shallow waters). The important new development in port operations that occur about five decades ago was the virtual disappearance of the true passenger liners; the cruise industry has emerged to replace it. Today, the passenger trade exists basically on local lines on inland waterways and between coastal ports. Cruise vessels, to date, have continued to look like liner vessels, not-withstanding that speed is no longer of paramount importance. The new ideas in port operations will bring new engineering and construction ideas in their wake. As pointed out by Hochstein, the nontechnical aspects of port performance, such as commercialization, liberalization, and privatization, along with improvements of port administration will continue to contribute to the institutional restructuring and drastic improvements in port operations. Commercialization gives to the port authorities' freedom similar to the private sector where decision making is decentralized and management is held accountable for port performance. Liberalization lessens the port authorities' monopoly on power by allowing the private sector to provide similar services and is complementary to commercialization. Privatization transfers functions previously performed by the port authority (government) to private sector. It may involve transfer of full or partial ownership of port facilities, or it may be limited to private sector management practices for the provision of port services via lease and operating contracts. Privatization usually associates with eliminated subsidies and reduced costs of port operation. The privatization of ports brings greatly enhanced commercial freedom to port managers and is recognized as one way to react more positively to market opportunities and use human incentives, based on personal gains and improvements, to increase efficiency of the port operations.

This trend is natural and will continue both in developed and developing countries. It must be recognized, however, that ports and harbours are built and operate within a certain societal framework that includes an array of political, financial, environmental, and other considerations.

Therefore, the port planner must have a clear understanding of local technical and nontechnical issues. For example, in some developing countries, existing or new ports are not solely an industrial development but also enterprises aimed at solving some regional, social, or demographical problems. Therefore, a careful approach to port privatization is needed in developing countries. The latter assumes that although commercial spirit there must not be discouraged, the commercial approach to port operations in some developing countries should not pursue a short-term financial gain.

In Europe, port privatization was successfully introduced in the 1980s in the United Kingdom where it accelerated in the 1990s. Also, today it is most apparent in Asia. Improvement of port administration encompasses actions that improve the performance of the organization. It may include corporate planning and carrier development, as well as installation and constant modernization of a computerized management information systems that enhances management without changing the port's institutional structure. Recent experience in ports worldwide suggest that commercialization and privatization are the most far-reaching and effective strategies to achieve the objective of port effectiveness.

In conclusion to this section, it should be noted that the future is not possible without thorough familiarity with the past which is a true foundation for new ideas. As it is rightfully said, "The past is not just something out of date, it is a record of human experience-an experience is certainly something which should be used to help shape the future."

The primary construction materials that were used for construction of older marine facilities were wood and stone. They were worked by hand and used for construction of sheet-pile bulkheads, piled piers, quay walls, breakwaters, and other structures. Wooden sheet piles and regular piles were driven by using primitive power equipment, and stone was placed from crude construction platforms. More than five centuries ago the Phoenicians extensively used wooden sheet piles and piles for construction of their marine facilities. For sheet-piling they used long planks made from Lebanon cedar. Various types of timber sheet-piling techniques (e.g., tongue and groove, laminated, and others) were used.

These piles were driven successively edge to edge to form a vertical wall for the purpose of preventing the retained materials from spreading and from being undermined by the action of waves and current.

Picture 1.11 (a) Wooden Sheet Pile (b) Breakwater

This type of construction was also known to ancient Egyptians and Romans. The Phoenicians also used heavy blocks locked together with copper dowels for construction of the open-sea port at Tyre and Sidon. This type of construction was also used by the Romans. In the 1800s, both materials still played a major role in port construction.

A great variety of gravity-type walls constructed from rubble masonry or heavy granite or limestone blocks have been built during the late 19th century. The history of heavy blockwork construction is traced back to ports in Mediterranean, at Marseilles and Algiers, with much of this pioneering work being carried out at the Port-of-Bonqie, Algeria where a quay wall composed of limestone blocks had been built as far back as 1840. During the same period of time, wood was extensively used for the construction of piled wharves and piers, as well as for gravity-type quays comprised of floated-in timber cribs with or without a masonry superstructure.

Picture 1.12 Floated-in timber cribs without superstructure

It should be noted that improved and economically sound blockwork quay walls are still in use. Today, timber cribs are used where wood is in abundance, and timber sheet-pile bulkheads made from treated wood have been constructed elsewhere, particularly in coastal regions as a secondary line of shore defence in ocean-exposed locations and for construction of low-height marine structures in small-craft harbours. In countries like India and Gulf region this is done by using concrete piles in most of the cases. Well-treated timber sheeting is also employed in permanent structures where it is always hidden under water, thus preserved from rot, and at locations where there are no marine organisms (e.g., borers (termites, etc.)) which can destroy wood. The same is true for wooden piles.

Cast-iron piles became complementary to timber piling in the early 1800s. The earliest reported use of iron sheet piles was construction of the North Pier of Bridlington harbour, the United Kingdom, in the early 1820s. Various types of iron sheet-pile sections were available at that time, and a considerable amount of exploratory work was carried out in order to develop the most economical profile. Cast iron, however, as a material had limitations primarily because of its vulnerability to brittle fracture during driving in hard soils. Typically, wrought-iron piles were used in a composite riveted form and were based primarily on the fitting of plates between suitable guides or against supports.

In 1897 a Danish engineer, Larssen, revolutionized the use of iron sheet piles by introducing a new pile section which was developed from a rolled through section plus a riveted "z" section, to form an interlock; this shape is very familiar in modern construction. In 1914 Larssen also introduced the first deep-arch section in which interlocks were situated in the neutral axis of the complete section; thus, their material bulk did not influence the bending moment to be taken up. Larssen's inventions and modifications helped to greatly increase the capacity and effectiveness of sheet piles in their ability to resist earth and water pressures. Increased pile stiffness enabled it to be driven without buckling or springing under the blows of the driving hammer, increased water-tightness of the sheeting prevented seepage through the wall, and most importantly, efficient use of rolling mills produced an economical section with interlocks.

At the beginning of this century, both wood and iron have been replaced by steel and reinforced concrete. The first sheet pile ever made from a rolled section was used in Chicago in 1901; it was called the Jackson pile. This was followed by the rather fast development of numerous straight or trough sections of steel piles that were produced around the world, either with integral locking arrangements or with a separate interlocking member. The first steel "z"-shaped sheet piling known as the Hoesch system was introduced in Belgium in 1913. In comparison with other sections, this type of piling was stiffer and had a higher section modulus at equal weight with other piling systems. Since this time, various combinations of different piling systems and various types of box piles (H-section) have been introduced in North America and Europe. At present, a variety of high-strength sheet pile sections are available from different pile manufacturers.

In addition to the above-mentioned piles, relatively low sectional modulus straight web steel sheet piles are often used in marine application for construction of cellular-type bulkheads. These piles were first manufactured and used in the United States in 1908/1909. It should be noted that steel pipe-type sheet piles are now coming into widespread use for deep water construction where a sheeting of greater strength is required. Reinforced concrete sheet piles have been used in harbour construction since the beginning of last century. They are usually considered relatively maintenance-free components of a sheet-pile wall.

Although many different design types have been developed and used in the past 50 or so years, the straight web piling bar provided with a tongue and groove, similar to that used on timber piles, is the most commonly used.

Since the 1950s, prestressed concrete sheet piles have replaced almost completely the ones made from regular reinforced concrete. Prestressing of concrete sheet-pile reinforcement has an advantage, especially in seawater environment, as cracking of concrete in the tension zone is thereby largely eliminated and the danger of corrosion of reinforcement is decreased.

The same applies to regular concrete piles that are extensively used in marine application. The advantage of piled structures is that they enable practically free passage of waves, which makes them particularly attractive for construction of the deep-water offshore terminals. A great variety of concrete and steel piles have been developed and used from the beginning of this century. The most significant development in this area is the use of large-diameter (up to 3.0 m and more), very long (60 m and longer) prestressed concrete and steel cylindrical piles. Depending on geotechnical site conditions, these piles can be installed by different methods (e.g., driven by hammer, vibrator, hydraulically, or a combination of some of these). It should be pointed out that the vibratory hammers introduced in the fifties and sixties changed the basic way piles had been driven since the late 1800s. New hydraulically operated hammers enable the constructors to drive piles under water. Similarly, very large floating and jack-up pile-driving equipment was developed and used for pile installation at exposed offshore locations. An array of piles with enhanced bearing capacities have been developed; for example, screw piles of different designs, prefabricated piles with enlargements on their shafts, belled piles, and other have been successfully used in port and offshore construction.

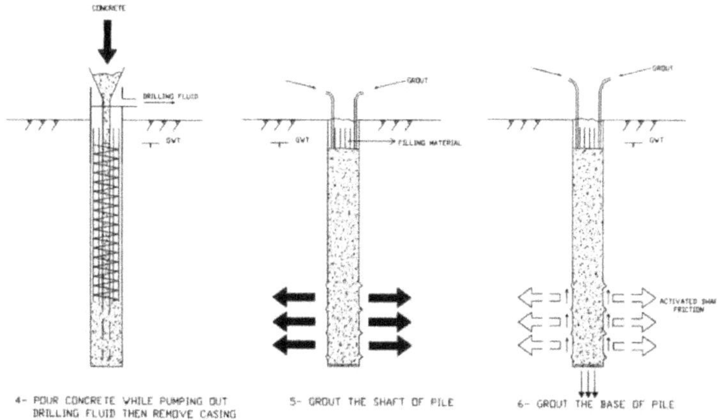


Picture 1.13 Details of a pile construction

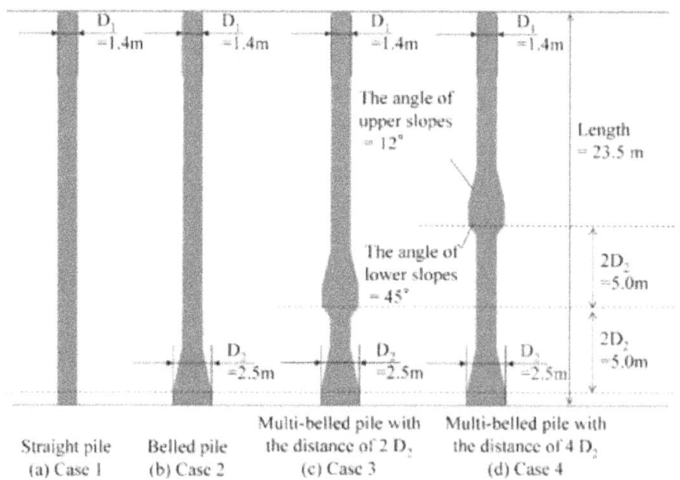


Picture 1.14 Types of Piles

High-strength steel and prestressed concrete allow the port designers and constructors the flexibility to design for greater depth, longer spans and higher capacity. For example, general cargo wharves are now routinely designed for 5.0 tonnes/m$^2$, up from 2.0 tonnes/m$^2$ 70-80 years ago. Galvanization and the use of protective coatings, such as epoxy, which came into use in the 1950s increased the longevity of marine structures. Epoxies are also used by constructors for splicing concrete structural elements in the field.

Remarkable progress has been achieved in concrete technology. Today's structural concrete is indeed a mixture of admixtures. Products such as superplasticizers, retarders, accelerators, air entrainers, and others allow concrete pours in cold temperature or hot weather. A denser and higher quality product is obtained by use of silica fume in a slurry or powdered form. Silica fume can substantially increase strength and density of concrete and make it virtually impervious to chloride penetration in the harsh marine environment. Furthermore, use of corrosion inhibitors may slow down the potential onset of corrosion in steel reinforcing bars.

Development of huge floating heavy lift equipment revolutionized the construction of gravity-type quay walls and breakwaters. These structures, generally built in water depths of 6-9 m in the late 1800s, are now constructed at depths of 25 m and below.

Finally, it should be pointed out that in the past 30-40 years primitive fenders used for protection of marine structures from ship impact have been replaced by very efficient high-energy-absorbing and low-reaction force rubber fender systems. At the present time, fender units are manufactured from solid and laminated rubber in different shapes and sizes. They are also manufactured in the form of a low-pressure inflated balloon (pneumatic fenders), or as a closed-cell foam filled unit. The pneumatic fender units have been manufactured up to 4.0 m in diameter and 12.0 m long.

Picture 1.15 (a) Fixed Type Fender

Picture 1.15 (b) Floating Type Fender

In modern marine engineering practice, a number of innovative and economical gravity-type quay walls have been employed. Among them are concrete large diameter floated-in caissons, bottomless concrete cylinders, and prefabricated L-shaped retaining walls of miscellaneous designs. An economical solution to gravity wall construction in the wet was also achieved by use of the traditional structures such as a large-diameter steel sheet-pile cell, a conventional box-like floated-in concrete caisson, and blockwork walls of enhanced designs. The economy of gravity wall construction was significantly improved by using innovative methods of bed preparation and placement and densification of backfill materials.

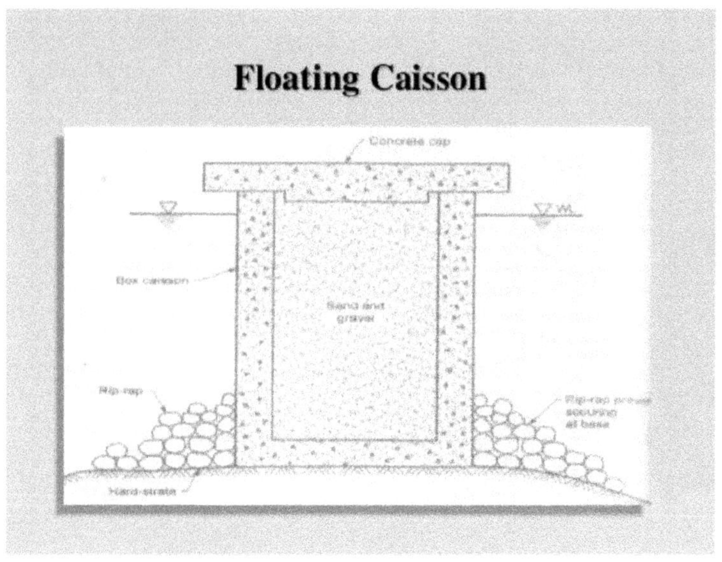


Picture 1.16 (a) Details of a Floating Caisson Foundation

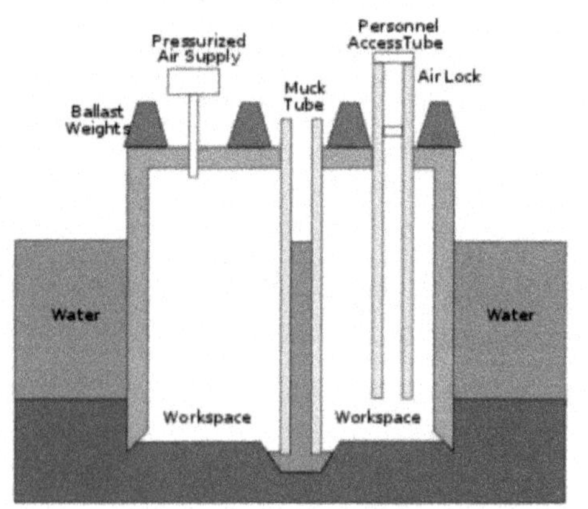


Picture 1.16 (b) Details of a Walled Caisson Foundation

Picture 1.16 (c) Open Caisson Foundation

Waterfront construction was accelerated by the use of prefabricated structural components. Prefabrication dramatically reduced the time required for overwater construction and enhanced quality and therefore longevity of marine structures. The design of any project is a continuous process, which begins with the perception of a need or opportunity, followed by a feasibility study that usually includes a conceptual design, and embedded by the detail design. The latter is followed by the construction of the project with subsequent commissioning. Furthermore, where required to support the basic concept of the project (e.g., harbour layout) or permit innovative structural designs to be used with confidence, research is undertaken. In the past, port and its related marine structures have been designed with a high degree of redundancy, largely because of the relatively rapid deterioration rate of structural materials in the marine environment, but also due to a lack of proper understanding of wave mechanics, mechanisms of ship-structure and/or soil-structure interaction. The latter was particularly true in designing a "flexible" structure such as sheet-pile bulkheads.

In the past 50 years, substantial progress has been achieved in such areas as the development of new, much stronger and more durable structural materials, the introduction of better construction technology, and a better understanding of the process of soil-structure interaction. Thus, research and development directly or indirectly became the integral part of the design process. The design of port layout with its related structures such as breakwaters, piers, and quay walls normally involve a great number of parameters that are generally considered to be far beyond the ability of purely analytical methods to achieve the reliable solution. This has been overcome by use of large-scale physical models, which appear to be a viable tool in solving a complex multiparameter problem.

Today's engineers have abundant analytical capability supported by computers. The mathematical modelling of a complex phenomenon such as the interaction between nature and engineering developments has become common-place in the design process. It enables the engineer to closely predict the behaviour of the complex structure in practice. For complex, projects, both mathematical and physical models are best used in combination. However, despite the prediction of model studies, the designer should exercise the proper level of conservative engineering judgment which is dictated by the complexity of marine foundations, marine environment, ship manoeuvres, and so on. Today, port and harbour engineering has entered the electronic age. The computer vastly enhances an engineer's productivity and his/her opportunities for innovative design. In addition to reducing the opportunities for making errors, the use of computers drastically enhances engineering judgment. By taking advantage of the speed of computer analysis, the engineer can explore a number of design alternatives in a short period of time. Today, computer hardware and software allow the engineer to see his project from all perspectives, investigate each detail, make changes by shaping as a sculptor might, then, when all is finished, have the calculations and drawings produced.

Computer-aided design and drafting (CAD) open opportunities for transition from traditional two-dimensional (2-D) design to three-dimensional (3-D) design. This has been made feasible by the rapid advances in computer-graphics hardware which permits full 3-D CAD models to be displayed quickly and effectively, with hidden lines removed or with shading; 3-D computer models can be viewed from any angle and viewpoint, in orthographic, isometric, perspective, or cutaway views. This helps to make the project aesthetically more acceptable to the community and overcome the public resistance to some projects regarded as a "visual pollution" to the area.

The importance of aesthetic aspects of any project now is fully recognized by the designers and developers, and the 3-D approach to structural and civil design helps to bridge the gap between art and science. Unfortunately, computerization of the design process has its own drawbacks; it provides not only the leading-edge technology but have been also a major source of concern. The popularity of computers has resulted in a flood of software, and on today's software market, there are nearly as many computer programs as there are researchers. Unfortunately, the quality of some software presently available on the market is questionable, and it would be of great interest and perhaps shock to some when results of analyses of certain structures are compared with the same input data using different programs.

The difference in the software output happens because some developers of computer software blindly rely solely on the mathematical approach to solving the problem and are ignorant about current state-of-the-art knowledge. Sometimes problems with software (e.g., incorrect sign convention) may cause a computer to subtract stresses when it must be added can be difficult to detect. Growing reliance on computer-aided analysis and design without adequate controls on misuse can lead to structural failures.

Recognizing this as a potential problem, the Committee on Practices to Reduce Failures, under the American Society of Civil Engineers Technical Council on Forensic Engineering, prepared a monograph titled "Avoiding Failures Caused by Misuse of Civil Engineering Software." The monograph, publicised in 1996, examined all computer-related issues where misuse could result in catastrophic failures, poor performance of facilities, and poor solutions to problems in civil engineering. Due to a worsening legal climate for practicing engineers, the designers are often not willing to accept potential risk associated with a more economical or innovative design. The conservative approach, which limits innovations in design and construction practices, causing economic problems, has been especially visible in foundation engineering. This has been explained by the uncertainties in soil-structure interaction and usually limited information on foundation soils available to the designer.

In the past 45-50 years, this has been improved by the extensive research into statistics and risk analysis, as applied to the field of geotechnical engineering. Also, the observational (monitored decisions) method, which provides the designer with flexibility in the decision-making process, has been introduced. Statistics provide procedures for obtaining information from given quantitative measurements, which, in turn, permits analysis of how the aforementioned listed uncertainties of soil and other parameters involved in soil-structure interaction may affect the design of the structure. Risk analysis is a set of decision-making procedures dealing with difficult design circumstances, where many components interact such that there is more than one mode of failure; and the observation method is a departure from the traditional design process in geotechnical/foundation engineering, because it allows one to make a final decision on foundation design in the future, both during construction when uncertainty in foundation soils became understood and during facility operation. The latter is particularly important where long-term changes in soil-structure interaction are expected.

Several advancements in port engineering have been pointed out in this section and the reader will find much more elsewhere in this book. Finally, it should be noted that in the past in order to reduce the cost of a design, attempts to standardize construction of marine structures were made. It has been proved, however, that standard designs to meet various site conditions, in general, and marine facilities, in particular, are not economical. In general, it is because the cost of the waterfront structure is so high that it would be false economy to attempt to reduce design costs by limiting the scope of design studies.

In conclusion, it must be said that producing a good, sound, and effective design is, of course, science; however, it is also an art. Just as an artist does, the designer must be imaginative in developing the concept of his or her project and, as a scientist, careful and meticulous in paying attention to all details.

# 2. Harbours

As navigation developed, ships felt the necessity to find shelter during their cruise and thus arose the creation of havens, where ships could take in and discharge, passengers and cargo, under protected conditions. Such a place of refuge is called a Harbour. As methods of navigation improved, these vessels gradually increased in size, number and importance; then arose the imperative need for providing suitable and spacious accommodation. Harbours are broadly classified as:

(1) Natural, and

(2) Artificial.

**Natural harbour:** Natural formations affording safe discharge facilities for ships/boats on sea coasts, in the form of creeks and basins are called Natural harbours. With the rapid development of navies engaged either in commerce, or war, improved accommodation and facilities for repairs, storage of cargo and connected amenities had to be provided in natural harbours.

**Artificial harbours:** Where such natural facilities are not available, countries having a sea board had to create or construct such shelters making use of engineering skills and methods and such harbours are called Artificial harbours. Artificial harbours are frequently built for use as ports. The oldest artificial harbour known is the Ancient Egyptian site at Wadi Al-Jarf, on the Red Sea coast, which is at least 4500 years old (ca. 2600-2550 BCE, reign of King Khufu). The largest artificially created harbour is Jebel Ali in Dubai.

A naval vessel could obtain shelter during bad weather within a tract or area of water close to the shore, providing a good hold for anchoring, protected by natural or artificial harbour walls against the fury of storms-such good berthing conditions constitute a roadstead. Such roadstead's could be naturally available or artificially created.

**Natural roadstead's:** (i) A deep navigable channel with a protective natural bank or shoal to seaward is a good example of a natural roadstead as shown in figure below.

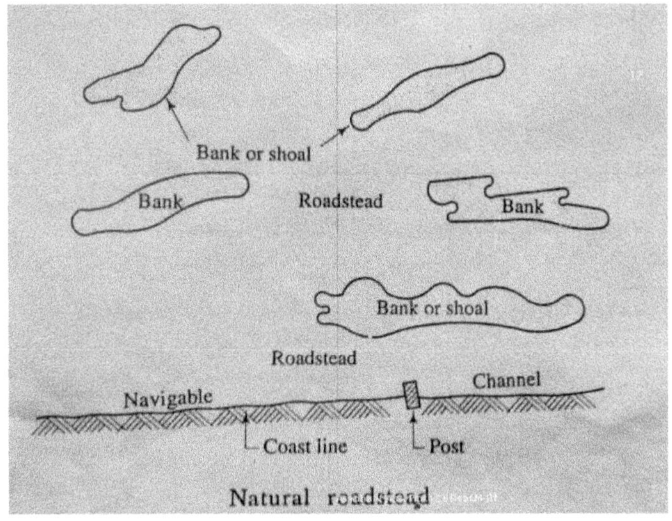


Picture 2.1 Natural roadstead.

(ii) A confined area naturally enclosed by islands as in a creek if available is known as a circumscribed natural roadstead.

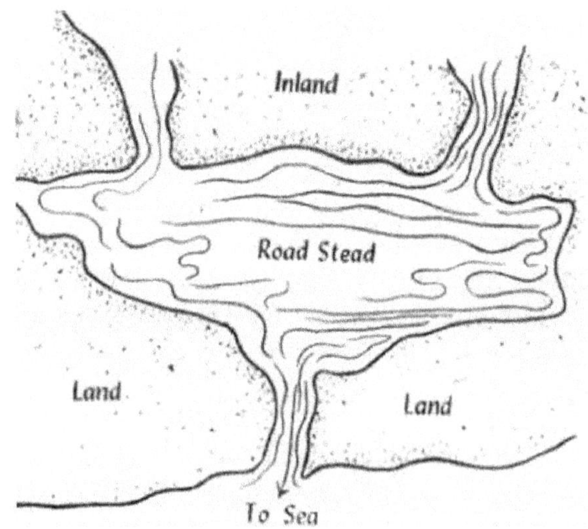


Picture 2.2 Naturally circumscribed roadstead

**Artificial roadstead's:** (i) These may be created suitably by constructing a break water or wall parallel to the coast or curvilinear from the coast. As an alternative a circumscribed Artificial roadstead could be formed by enclosing a tract providing good anchorage, by projecting solid walls called jetties from the shore.

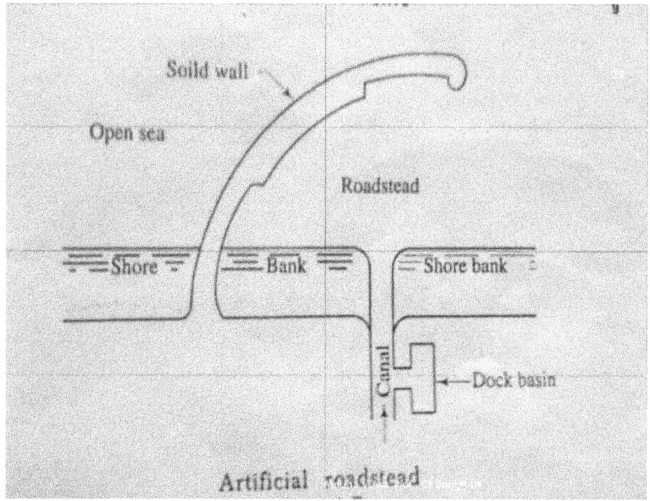


Picture 2.3 Artificial roadstead's

Picture 2.4 Artificial Roadsteads (Palm Island-Dubai)

Picture 2.5 Artificially circumscribed roadstead

(ii) Another method is to create a confined basin of small area having a narrow entrance and exit for ships. Such roadstead's with smaller inner enclosures and wharf and with loading and unloading facilities are commonly provided for fishing vessels.

Picture 2.6 Confined Basin

From their utility and situation harbours are further classified into three major types, i.e.,

(i) Harbours of refuge including Naval bases.

(ii) Commercial harbours, connected with ports.

(iii) Fishery harbours.

It is necessary to study the requirements of these types and provide for them.

Requirements of harbour of refuge:

(i) Ready accessibility.

(ii) Safe and commodious anchorage.

(iii) Facilities for obtaining supplies and repairs.

On dangerous coast-lines, disabled or damaged ships, under stress of weather conditions will need quick shelter and immediate repairs. All types of naval craft, small and big will need refuge in an emergency and hence such refuge harbours should provide commodious accommodation. Modern big ships require a lot of elbow room for purposes of manoeuvring or turning about.

Requirements of commercial harbour:

(i) Spacious accommodation for the mercantile marine.

(ii) Ample quay space and facilities for transporting, loading and unloading cargo.

(iii) Storage sheds for cargo.

(iv) Good and quick repair facilities to avoid delay.

(v) More sheltered conditions as loading and unloading could be done with advantage in calmer waters.

Commercial harbours could be situated on coasts or estuaries of big rivers or even on inland river coasts.

They do not normally have any emergency demand like a harbour of refuge and practically the size and number of ships using such harbours are known factors.

Requirements of fishing harbour:

(i) Harbour should be constantly open for departure and arrival of fishing ships.

(ii) Loading and unloading facilities and quick despatch facilities for the perishable fish catch like railway sidings and roads.

(iii) Refrigerated stores with ample storing space for preserving the catch.

Accessibility and size of harbours: Accessibility depends on the location of the harbour.

The harbour entrance should be designed and located for quick easy negotiation by ships, overtaken by storms. At the same time, it should be narrow enough not to expose the harbour to the effects of the stormy sea. Maximum dimensions up to 500 metres have been adopted. The entrance is generally placed to receive the ship direct from the worst storm affected part of the sea, with a passage to the interior of the harbour so arranged to minimise the effect of rough seas.

Size of harbour depends upon the number and size of ships likely to use the harbour at one time.

Some of the biggest modern ships are 300m to 500m long and over a 120m wide and there should be sufficient area to manoeuvring them, without collision. Thus, the size is determined by,

(i) Accommodation required.

(ii) Convenience for manoeuvring and navigation.

(iii) Adaptability to natural features.

Regarding the entrance width the narrower the entrance the better is the interior protection, consistent with easy and quick entry or exit of the biggest vessel using the harbour. Even when the break waters are high enough to protect the harbour, waves from outside the harbour, set up very small waves inside the harbour depending on the entrance widths.

# 3. Tides, Winds and Waves

The harbour engineer has to study certain natural and meteorological phenomena which primarily affect the location and design of the harbour. They are:

(i) Coastal currents and evidences of silting, including Littoral drift or Coast erosion.

(ii) Tides and tidal range.

(iii) Wind, Wave and their combined effect on Harbour structures.

**Littoral Drift:** On exposed coasts - the shore line undergoes gradual and continual change. Such changes consist of erosion or washing away at certain sections, while in other sections accretion or deposition takes place. This process of carrying away and depositing materials, is caused by current low created by waves impinging on the shore line. These waves are introduced by prevailing winds and tend to stir up and move the lighter particles of sand in suspension. The general effect of wind is shown in picture3.1. It tends to carry the drifting sand in a zig zag line.

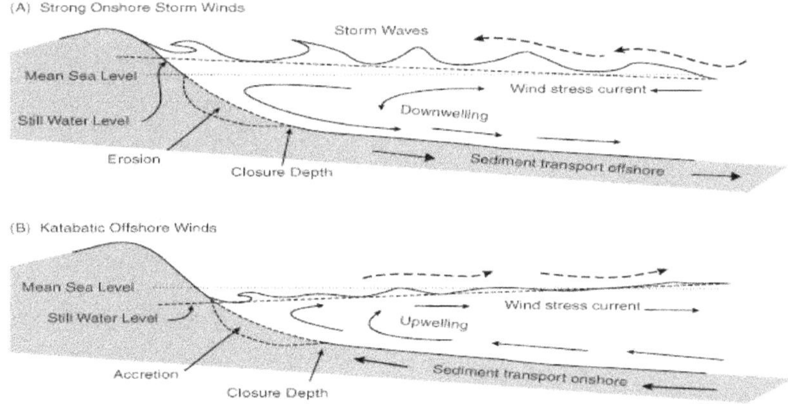

Picture 3.1 Wind effect and movement on shore

The process of movement and deposition are complex. Such sand drifts occurring in the proximity of foreshores is known as 'littoral drift'. This factor is important in choosing proper harbour sites on exposed shores.

**Tides:** Tides on the coast-line are caused by the sun and moon. The effect of tides is to artificially raise and lower the mean sea level during certain stated periods of the day. This apparent variation of mean sea level is known as the tidal range. Allowance will have to be made for this variation in designing and constructing maritime structures, regular tide charts are prepared for consultation in important coastal sections.

**Spring tides and Neap tides:** Tides, are well known rises and falls of the surface of the sea and of some rivers caused by attraction of the Sun and Moon. There are usually two rises or flood tides and two falls or ebbs or low tides every 24 hrs. 50 min. (Lunar day). But the intervals of ebb and flow are subject to great variations, as also the height of tides at the same place. These irregularities are owing to the shape of coast-line, depth of water, winds and other causes.

Usually at new and full moon or rather a day or two after (or twice in each lunar month) the tides rise higher and fall lower than at other times and these are called Spring tides. Also, one or two days after the moon is in her-quarters (twice in a lunar month) the tides rise and fall less than at other times and are then called Neap tides. The total height of spring tides is general 1.5 to 2 times as great as that at neaps.

**Waves and wind:** The 'sea wave' is by far the most powerful force acting on harbour barriers and against which the engineer has to contend. This is produced by the joint action of wind and water and has tremendous damaging power. It is a most incomprehensible natural phenomenon. The formation of storm waves takes place in the open sea, due to the action of wind.

Water waves are of two kinds; viz., waves of oscillation and waves of translation - the former are stationary, while the latter possess forward motion. But all translatory waves originally start as waves of oscillation and become translatory by further wind action. The Harbour engineer's main concern is the translatory wave. The wave movement and its breaking on the beach or shore is shown in picture 3.1 above.

The movement of a translatory particle of water of the wave as it nears the shore or obstruction is such as to make the crest gain on the trough causing a steeper and steeper crest, which overhangs and falls down with a bang and breaks into froth. It is in this phase the wave constitutes a potent disruptive force.

Any unevenness of the sea bed or natural and artificial protrusions on it are capable of breaking up the wave on its travel. Even a current of air introduced from the bed upwards disperses the wave. This is done by introducing a perforated pipe along the bottom of the sea, (when storms are anticipated) before hand and discharge compressed air just when the translatory motion commences. Such an arrangement is known as an 'air brake water' and has been tried with success in the U.S.A, during storms in Pacific Ocean. The height of waves generated in the area rose to 15 feet, but when compressed air started discharging, the air bubbles broke up the waves into harmless small ripples. Also, islands and jutting pieces of land divert the direction of waves and deflect them into shallow ground and so break their power of damage (picture3.2).

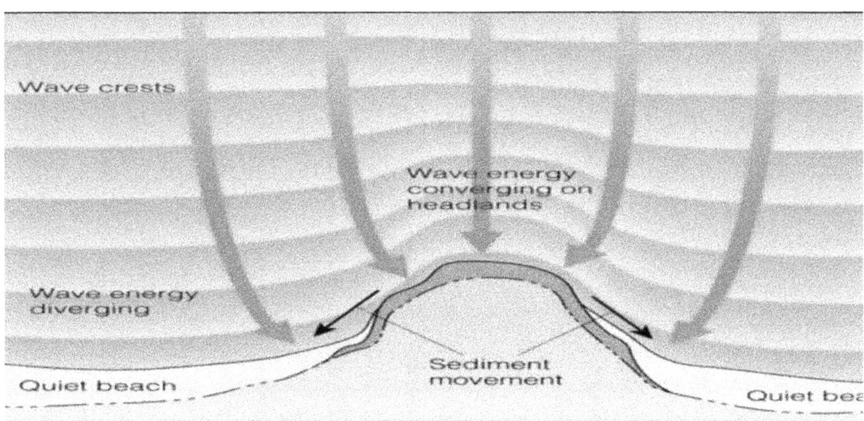


Picture3.2 Deflecting of wave by Head land

**Height and length of waves:** Waves being generated by wind; their development depends upon the surface area of sea exposed to wind action. The great length and height attained by waves are largely based on this effective surface area. Such a surface giving rise to a wave is called a 'Fetch' and is usually measured in miles" denoting the length across which the wave action is generated and is active.

The height of the wave in feet = $1{\cdot}5\sqrt{F}$, where F is the fetch in miles.

This is an empirical formula employed to ascertain the approximate value of the height of a wave. Another factor in determining the height is the location of harbour works in relation to the fetch and direction of wind. (For example, at Mumbai harbour the fetch is nearly 500 miles of open sea, and the depth is very great. During the peak of south west monsoon, the highest wave was found to be not more than 18 feet in height. The reason for this is attributable, to the fetch being probably at right-angles to the direction of wind.)

Waves cannot attain full height in shallow waters. No wave can have a height greater than the depth of water through which it passes. This is the reason why, intervention of undulations in the bed reduces the depth of wave at the section.

**Length of wave:** The length could be defined as the distance between crests of a wave (picture 3.3). The length influences the force of the wave. It is difficult to estimate the length in open sea and is generally computed by Bertin's formula, as:

$$L = \left(\frac{t^2}{2\pi}\right) g \text{ feet}$$

Or, $L = 5{\cdot}125\, t^2$ feet.

Where L = length in feet and $t$ is the period in seconds for two successive waves to pass the same section.

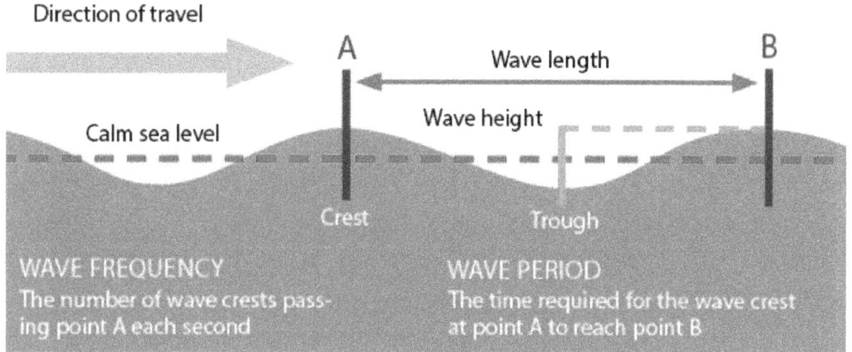


Picture 3.3 Length and Height of Wave

The length of the wave, with the water depth, determines the velocity of the particles of water in the wave. Lengths have been known to reach a maximum of 600 feet to 1000 feet. The height of storm waves on various important water way" have been observed to be as follows:

| | |
|---|---|
| North Sea | 12' to 15' |
| Mediterranean | 15' to 20' |
| Atlantic Ocean | 30' to 40' |
| Pacific Ocean | 50' to 60' |
| Tropical Oceans | 50' to 60' |

Wave section: A sea wave when breaking against an obstacle or a sea structure gives rise to various forces, and the important ones of these are as follows:

(i) A direct horizontal force causing compression.

(ii) A deflected vertical force tending to shear away any projections on the face of the wall.

(iii) A downward vertical force due to the collapse of the wave, which tends the disturb the mound construction of the foundation and sea bed.

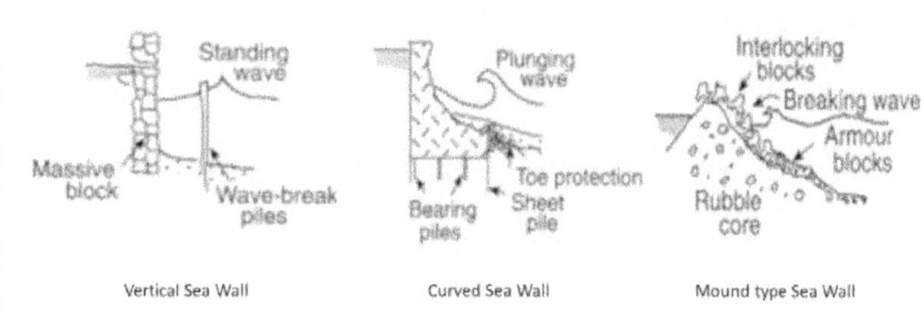


Picture 3.4 Wave Impact on different types of seawalls.

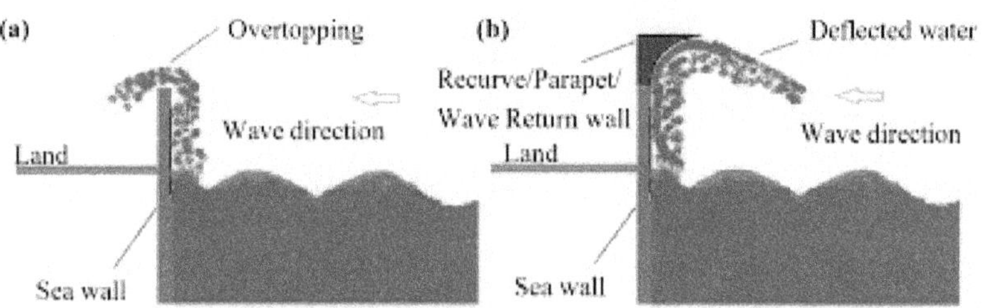


Picture 3.5 Forces action on sea-walls

(iv) A suction due to the return of the water after striking, which tends to disturb the mounds in foundation.

These forces have been diagrammatically shown in picture 3.5 acting on a sea wall with a rubble mound foundation.

Applying these fundamental forces in designing sea walls or break waters, they give rise to the following phenomena:

(i) A powerful momentary impact combined with a hydrostatic pressure for a short period.

(ii) A vibratory effect on the whole structure.

(iii) Impulses imparted to the water contained in the joints or pores producing internal pressures in various directions.

(iv) Alternate contraction and expansion of the confined air in the pores and cavities of the structure.

Theoretical evaluation of these forces or determination is practically impossible, but to guide the Engineer a few factors like (a) dynamic value of wave action, (b) air compression and (c) water hammer effect could be studied with advantage.

Dynamical effect of wave action: Based on the simple principles of dynamics, the reaction of a surface subjected to continued impacts could be measured by the rate of destruction of the momentum. The strike of the wave is sudden and continuous, and causes a sharp blow of high instantaneous intensity, followed by a static pressure for a very short period. Generally, the whole process is considered as a simple and constant impact.

The mass of water impinging on unit surface

$= \frac{(w.v)}{g}$,

Where w is the wt. of unit volume of water,

v, the velocity of the wave, and

g, acceleration due to gravity.

The rate of dissipation of momentum = $(\frac{(w.v)}{g})*v$

$= \frac{(w.v^2)}{g}$,

Therefore, the reaction of the surface on which the wave strikes = $\frac{(w.v^2)}{g}$ = p, the pressure on unit surface .....(1)

**(a) In deep water:** When the depth of water is great compared to the length of wave, velocity is utmost equal to that caused by a freely falling body through a height equal to half the radius of the circle the circumference of which constitutes the length of wave. Thus, velocity v = $\sqrt{(2g*\frac{l}{2\pi})}$

$= 2.25\sqrt{l}$ ...................... (2)

Considering the wave as a cycloidal curve, the height h of the wave

$= \frac{l}{\pi}$, where l is the length of the wave

: v = √4h from equation (2).

Substituting this value in equation (1), we get,

$p = 16 \frac{wh}{g}$

$= \frac{wh}{2}$ nearly.

**(b) In shallow water:** In shallow water, where if depth of water is d, it has been found the velocity v = 5· 73√d approximately.

Substituting this value of v in equation (1), we have p= $\frac{w}{g}$*32·8*d or wd approximately.

Hence if the depth is taken in terms of height of wave as equivalent to 3h, 2h or h, then corresponding values of p is 3wh, 2wh or wh respectively.

Air compression: The maximum internal pressure on an imprisoned air column in the pores or crevices of structures, will be equal to as much as 3:5 times the pressure of water on the face of the wall or structure. In crevices or open joints in masonry structures, this disruptive force, when repeated constantly, has a powerful damaging effect. But where such sea walls or break waters are constructed of the mound type the air compression is greatly reduced, owing to the numerous void spaces in the mound, through which the pressure relieves itself.

**(c) Water hammer:** This hydraulic phenomenon produces maximum pressures equivalent to fifteen times the face pressure on enclosed water columns, inside the joints and pores of the masonry structure, but if there is sufficient air cushion at the end of the opening, much of the effect is reduced. (picture 3.6).

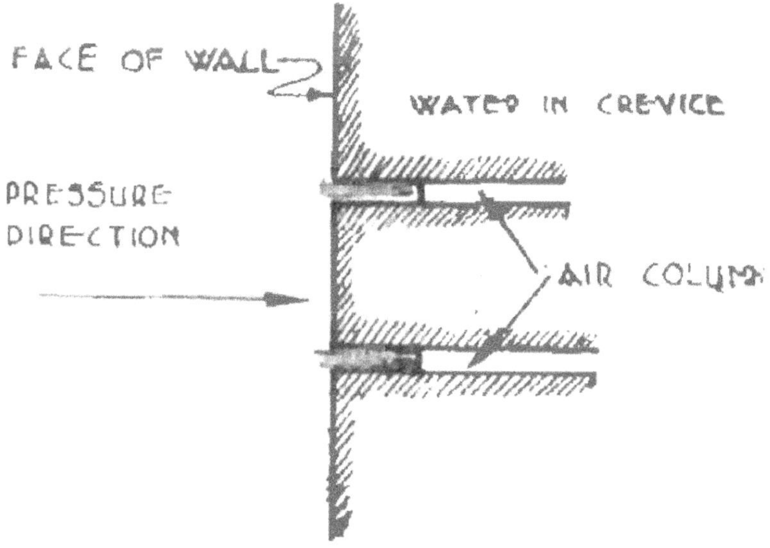


Picture 3.6 Water hammer and air cushion

A notable example to illustrate the incredible and unpredictable damage caused by sea waves, is that of Genoa harbour, where during a severe storm considerable damage and destruction was caused.

The harbour at that time had a rock and concrete break water roughly of the shape of letter Z in plan, and a 1.5km in length. The 'fetch' in the ' area is nearly 200 kilometres and the storm waves rose nearly 25' high. In the first section the waves had sucked away the boulder protection for a length of 800' exposing the foundation completely sweeping the apron stones each weighing about 40 tons a distance of 160 feet away from the wall.

Fig 3.7 Genoa Harbour

In the third section 500 feet length of wall was split into several sections and bodily thrown into the harbour, the largest such block weighing nearly 10 to 12 tons.

# 4. Break Waters

**Break water:** The protective barrier constructed to enclose harbour's, and to keep the harbour waters undisturbed by the effect of heavy and strong seas are called break waters. Such a construction makes it possible to use the area thus enclosed as a safe anchorage for ships and to facilitate loading of cargo in comparatively calm waters.

Sometimes the inner side of a break water is constructed as a Quay for cargo handling and is known as a Mole.

**Classification of break waters:** Break waters are classified mainly into: (i) Heap or mound break water, (ii) Mound with superstructure, (iii) Upright wall break water, (iv) Caisson, (v) Wave absorbing caisson, and (vi) Wave attenuator

(1) Heap or mound break water is a heterogeneous assemblage of natural rubble, undressed stone blocks, rip rap, supplemented in many cases by artificial blocks of huge bulk and weight, the whole being deposited without any regard to bond or bedding. This is the simplest type and is constructed by tipping or dumping of rubble stones into the sea till the heap or mound emerges out of the water, the mound being consolidated and its side" slopes regulated by the action of the waves. The quantity of rubble depends upon the depth, rise of tides and waves and exposure. On exposed sites the waves gradually drag down the mound, giving it a flat slope on the sea face. As far as possible such flattening has to be protected.

The disturbing action of the waves is most between the high and low water levels. Consequently, all protective methods are adopted above the low water level. Protection is also very necessary to the top of the mound and outer, or exposed face.

Methods of protection:

(a) Dumping heavy blocks of concrete on top and on front face. This to a great extent resists the flattening action of the waves, by sheer weight.

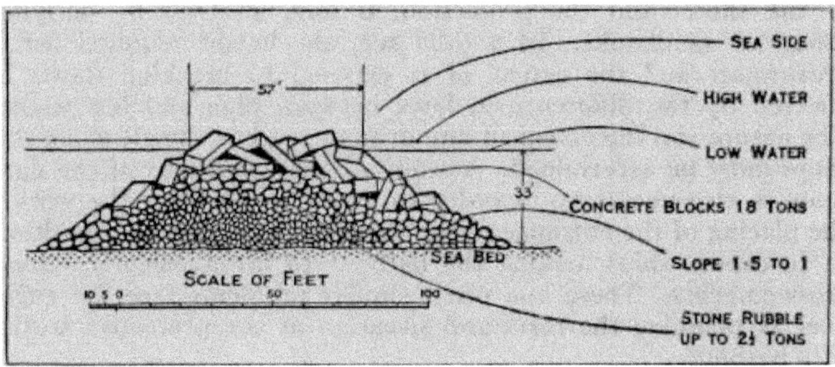


Picture 4.1 Concrete blocks on top and front face of breakwater

These blocks weigh 25 tons to 30 tons and are either deposited at random picture 4.1 or laid in courses as shown in picture 4.2. These blocks are prepared as rectangular solids and laid with ends towards the waves. This provides minimum area and maximum mass against impact or overturning.

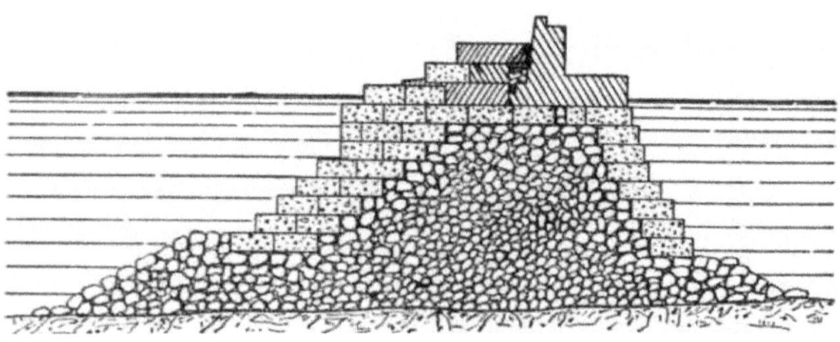

Picture 4.2 (a) & (b) Concrete blocks layed in regular courses for Breakwater

(b) Paving the upper part up to the low water level by deep granite blocks (picture 4.3) is another method to protect the top and face. Granite paving blocks set in cement mortar reduces the erosive action of the waves.

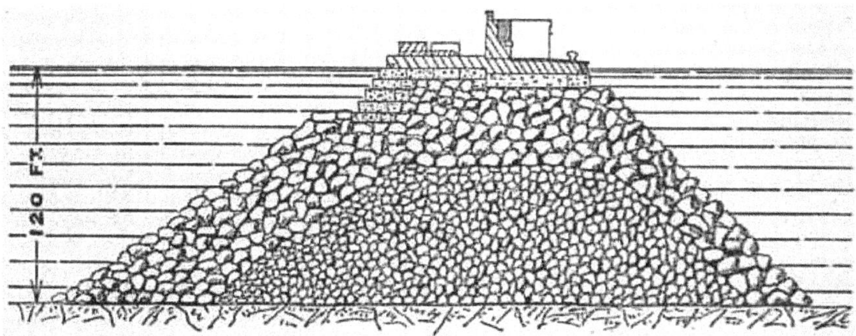


Picture 4.3 Top protection by Granite Paving for Breakwater

**Mound formation:** Rubble mounds are formed using rubble of assorted weights, placed according to sizes; the smallest and lightest materials constituting the core. The sizes are increased gradually outwards. This arrangement' is logical, exposing the bigger sizes to the action of the waves, while the smaller sizes forming the core are protected (see picture 4.4).

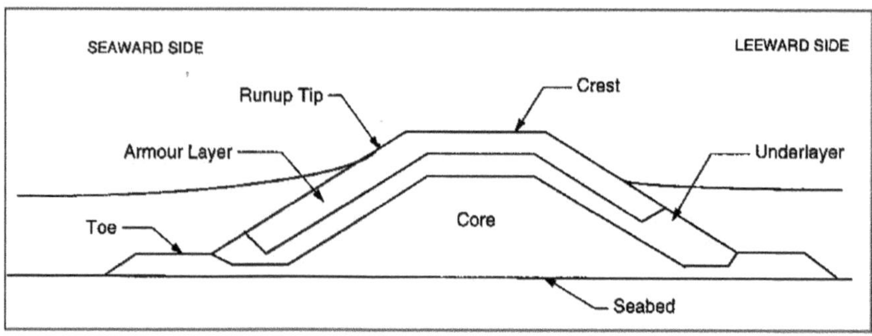


Picture 4.4 Mound Foundation Breakwater

Where rubble is difficult to get concrete blocks have been used to form the mound. Concrete blocks have the advantage that they could be heaped at a steeper slope than rubble, economizing in space and material. Also, the size of blocks could be controlled to suit the exposure condition.

(2) *(i) Mound with superstructure founded at low water:*

A solid superstructure consisting of a Quay protected by a parapet on the sea face is constructed on top of the rubble mound (picture 4.5). Such a construction is founded about low water level. The advantages of such a construction are,

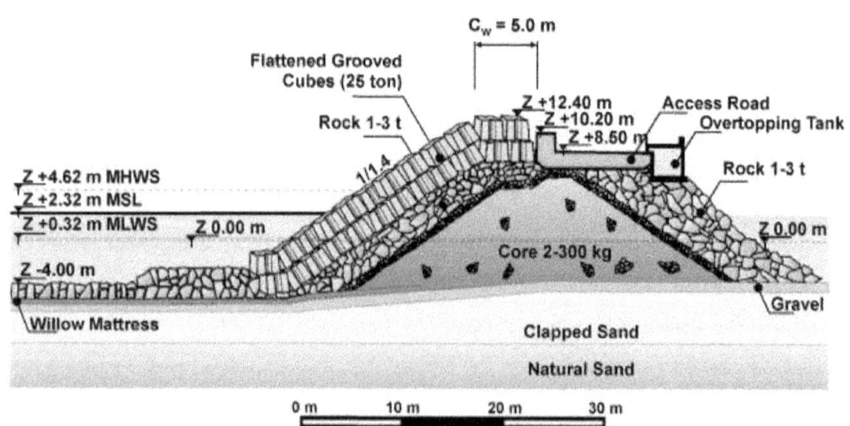


Picture 4.5 mound with solid superstructure and concrete block protection

(a) It provides a platform for handling cargo.

(b) It protects the top of the mound.

(c) It reduces the mass of rubble required for the mound in proportion to the depth at which it is founded.

Unlike the ordinary or plain mound break water, this type of construction makes it possible for ships to come close to the break water wall on the inner or harborside for loading and unloading cargo.

Heavy concrete blocks are used on the sea face for protection. The front batter changes from 2·8 to 1, abruptly to 1 to 1 in order to provide a sharp edge to cut the waves on impact.

*(ii) Mound with superstructure founded below L. W. level:*

This type of construction affords the advantage of founding the superstructure well below the level of disturbance, the waves having practically no disturbing effect at such low levels. In deep waters this type is very economical in mound material (picture 4.6).

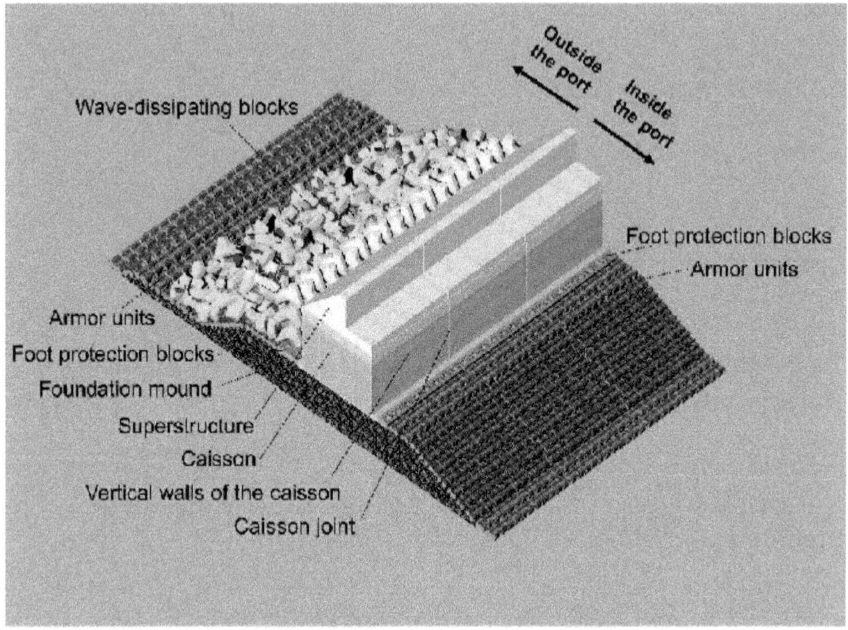


Picture 4.6 Mound with Superstructure foundation below L.W.L

**Stability of mounds**: Mounds lack quality of permanence in shape and section specially the upper portions. They stand in equilibrium, below levels of wave effect at slopes of 45° to 50°. The maximum wave effect and disturbance of the mound is felt between H.W.L. and L.W.L. Hence large and bigger blocks of 30 tons each or more are deposited at a slope of 1 to 1 in this region. The concrete blocks are made in large rectangular blocks and laid as headers, offering minimum face area and maximum resistance to overturning.

*(3) Caisson*

Caisson breakwaters typically have vertical sides and are usually erected where it is desirable to berth one or more vessels on the inner face of the breakwater. They use the mass of the caisson and the fill within it to resist the overturning forces applied by waves hitting them. They are relatively expensive to construct in shallow water, but in deeper sites they can offer a significant saving over revetment breakwaters.

An additional rubble mound is sometimes placed in front of the vertical structure in order to absorb wave energy and thus reduce wave reflection and horizontal wave pressure on the vertical wall. Such a design provides additional protection on the sea side and a quay wall on the inner side of the breakwater, but it can enhance wave overtopping.

*(4) Wave absorbing caisson*

A similar but more sophisticated concept is a wave-absorbing caisson, including various types of perforation in the front wall.

Such structures have been used successfully in the offshore oil-industry, but also on coastal projects requiring rather low-crested structures (e.g. on an urban promenade where the sea view is an important aspect (e.g. Beirut and Monaco)). In the latter, a project is presently ongoing at the Anse du Portier including 18 wave-absorbing 27 m (89 ft) high caissons.

*(5) Wave attenuator*

Wave attenuators consist of concrete elements properly dimensioned placed horizontally just one foot under the free surface, positioned along a line parallel to the coast. The wave attenuator has four sea-side (seaward) slabs, one vertical slab, and two rear-side (landward) slabs, each separated from the next by a space of 200 millimeters (7.9 in). This row of 4 front side slabs and two rear side slabs, reflects the offshore wave by the action of the volume of water located under it which, made to oscillate under the effect of the incident wave, creates waves in phase opposition to the incident wave downstream from the slabs.

## MOUND CONSTRUCTION:

*Size of material and arrangement:* Mounds are formed in assorted layers, the smaller sized material being dispose at the base and the larger at the top and sides, particularly between the High and Low water levels, which region is the worst affected (picture 4.4).

*Methods of construction:*

Mound construction is carried out by anyone of the following three methods.

(i) Barge method.

(ii) Staging method.

(iii) Low level method.

(1) *Barge method:* Special barges with flat bottoms and hoppers with vertical sides and doors at the bottom opening outwards are used. The hoppers are loaded with rubble, and the barge is adjusted and aligned in position along the line of construction and the load is discharged by opening the hopper doors (picture 4.7). Rubble should be evenly distributed over the entire width of base of the break water mound. The layers are trimmed and rectified to the correct section by divers.

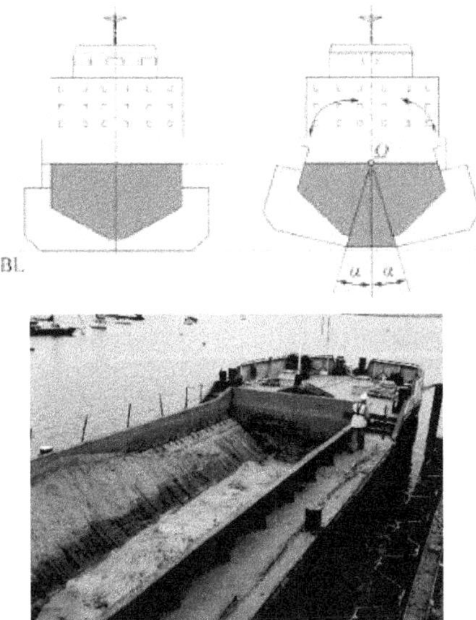


Picture 4.7 Discharge from Hopper Barge

When the mound rises up sufficiently high that hopper barges cannot be used, decked barges (picture 4.8) are resorted to. These are loaded and brought to the site and slightly canted by flooding compartments on one side, causing a tilt which dislodges the material.

This method has the advantage of offering the opportunity for a uniform depositing, simultaneously over a large area.

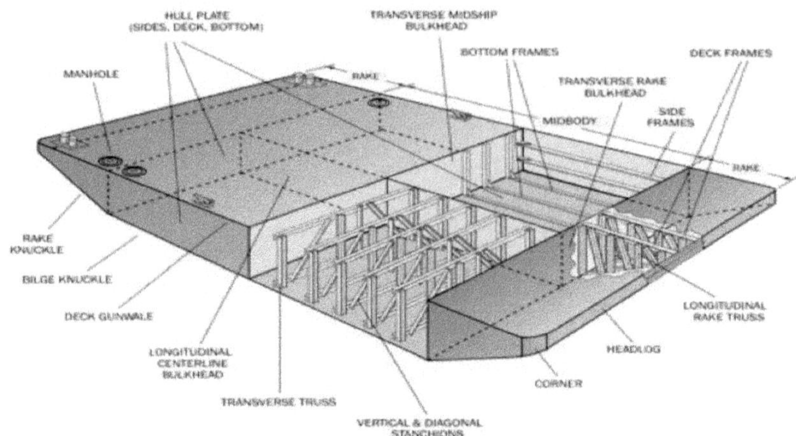


Picture 4.8 Deck Barge

(2) *Staging method:* A series of piles are driven at regular intervals of 15' to 20' and connected by longitudinal runners, struts and braces (picture 4.10) forming a number of parallel tracks for tipping wagons to move on rails. These tracks are well above the high sea level and at 25' to 35' centers. The material is hauled on this staging and is tipped at the ends and sides. As work in one section is completed the staging is removed and re-erected in a forward position to continue the work. Very heavy and powerful tackle arrangement is necessary to withdraw the staging piles from the areas where the mound has been completed.

Picture 4.9 Staging method for foundation

(3) *Low level method:* This consists in forming a length of mound from the shore, well above the high sea level and using this for laying tracks and running tipping wagons on this solid break water structure as it advances. This method naturally restricts the scope of a multi-section attack, but has the advantage of consolidating the mound formed, by the traffic of loaded wagons.

**Break water armour units**

As design Waves heights get larger, rubble mound break waters require larger armour units to resist the wave forces. These armour units can be formed of concrete or natural rock. The largest standard grading for rock armour units given in CIRIA 683 "The Rock Manual" is 10–15 tonnes. Larger gradings may be available, but the ultimate size is limited in practice by the natural fracture properties of locally available rock.

Shaped concrete armour units (such as Dolos, Xbloc, Tetrapod, etc.) can be provided in up to approximately 40 tonnes (e.g. Jorf Lasfar, Morocco), before they become vulnerable to damage under self weight, wave impact and thermal cracking of the complex shapes during casting/curing. Where the very largest armour units are required for the most exposed locations in very deep water, armour units are most often formed of concrete cubes, which have been used up to ~195 tonnes for the tip of the breakwater at Punta Langosteira near La Coruña, Spain.

Preliminary design of armour unit size often undertaken using the Hudson Equation, Van der Meer and more recently Van Gent et al.; these methods are all described in CIRIA 683 "The Rock Manual" and the United States Army Corps of Engineers Coastal engineering manual (available for free online) and elsewhere. For detailed design the use of scaled physical hydraulic models remains the most reliable method for predicting real-life behavior of these complex structures.

## Unintended consequences

Breakwaters are subject to damage and overtopping in severe storms. Some may also have the effect of creating unique types of waves that attract surfers, such as The Wedge at the Newport breakwater.

### *Sediment effects*

The dissipation of energy and relative calm water created in the lee of the breakwaters often encourage accretion of sediment (as per the design of the breakwater scheme). However, this can lead to excessive salient build up, resulting in tombolo formation, which reduces longshore drift shoreward of the breakwaters. This trapping of sediment can cause adverse effects down-drift of the breakwaters, leading to beach sediment starvation and increased coastal erosion. This may then lead to further engineering protection being needed down-drift of the breakwater development. Sediment accumulation in the areas surrounding breakwaters can cause flat areas with reduced depths, which changes the topographic landscape of the seabed.

Salient formations as a result of breakwaters are a function of the distance the breakwaters are built from the coast, the direction at which the wave hits the breakwater, and the angle at which the breakwater is built (relative to the coast). Of these three, the angle at which the breakwater is built is most important in the engineered formation of salients. The angle at which the breakwater is built determines the new direction of the waves (after they've hit the breakwaters), and in turn the direction that sediment will flow and accumulate over time.

*Environmental effects*

The reduced heterogeneity in sea floor landscape introduced by breakwaters can lead to reduced species abundance and diversity in the surrounding ecosystems. As a result of the reduced heterogeneity and decreased depths that breakwaters produce due to sediment build up, the UV exposure and temperature in surrounding waters increase, which may disrupt surrounding ecosystems.

But as a kind of environmental friendly breakwater, pile breakwaters because of occupation of a small area is not harmful to sea wildlife.

**Construction of detached breakwaters**

There are two main types of offshore breakwater (also called detached breakwater): single and multiple. Single, as the name suggests, means the breakwater consists of one unbroken barrier, while multiple breakwaters (in numbers anywhere from two to twenty) are positioned with gaps in between (160–980 feet or 50–300 metres). The length of the gap is largely governed by the interacting wavelengths. Breakwaters may be either fixed or floating, and impermeable or permeable to allow sediment transfer shoreward of the structures, the choice depending on tidal range and water depth. They usually consist of large pieces of rock (granite) weighing up to 10–15 tonnes each, or rubble-mound. Their design is influenced by the angle of wave approach and other environmental parameters. Breakwater construction can be either parallel or perpendicular to the coast, depending on the shoreline requirements.

# 5. Wall Break Water

These are regularly designed as structures subjected to forces causing failure in the following ways:

(i) By the shearing of bed joints or by sliding of one block against the other.

(ii) By overturning as a solid mass.

(iii) By the uplifting of horizontal layers.

(iv) By fracture.

**I. Shearing of bed joints due to horizontal pressure of the wave:** This is prevented by

(a) The resistance offered by the adhesive force of the mortar joint. Usually 1:3 cement mortar is used, giving a high adhesive strength of 6 to 7 tons/sqft.

(b) Frictional resistance to siding: In the case of concrete or stone blocks the coefficient of friction is 0·7. The resistance will be 0·7W. But the effective weight should be calculated after making allowance for loss of weight due to immersion, equal to the weight of an equal volume of water.

**II. Overturning:** It is another aspect of the horizontal pressure and the design should provide for this, like ordinary walls, to keep the resultant of the weight and the horizontal pressure within the middle third of the base, to avoid tensional stress in the foundation courses. The maximum permissible compressive stress is taken as 12 tons/sqft. with concrete on rock base.

The horizontal force causing shear of the joints and the overturning has been experimentally determined in many cases and the maximum value has been found to be about 2·8 tons/sq.ft. at mean sea level, taking the average wave size as 26' (picture 5.1).

Picture 5.1 Horizontal forces on Sea-wall

**III. Uplifting:** It is due to wave action or wave force underneath the mass. The only opposing force to eliminate this is the weight of the masonry, which thus is a simple case of equal and opposite forces.

**IV. Fracture:** This does not result directly from wave action. It may be caused by the dislocated blocks, knocking against each other, and breaking loose the joints, and such failures are usually avoided by proper bonding in the masonry, by joggles etc (see picture 5.2).

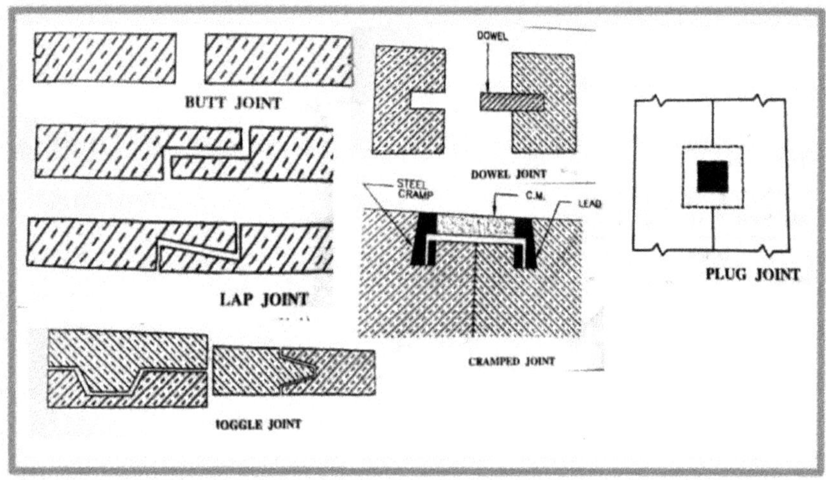


Picture 5.2 Types of joints in blocks

This type of break water construction is suited to sheltered site and not reliable for very heavy seas. When depth is not great and the bottom is firm upright wall break water could be built.

*Advantages:* (i) Reduces the amount of material.

(ii) Avoids dangers of unequal settlement, as in the case of mound.

*Disadvantages:* (i) Involves building a good height of wall under water.

(ii) Calls for special care and costly methods of construction.

A typical section of upright wall break water is shown in picture 5.3.

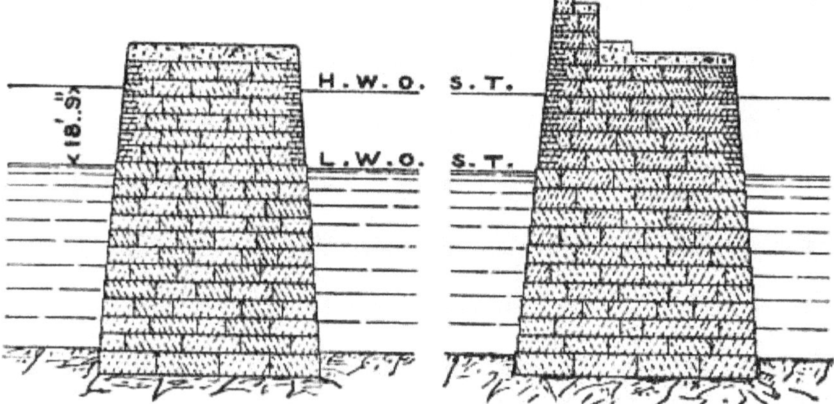


Picture 5.4 Section of upright wall break water

*Alternate construction:* 100-ton concrete bags are deposited by special hopper barges across the full width, up to L.W. Level. Above this level solid concrete wall is constructed. Jute cloth protects concrete during passage through water, and the cement mortar oozing out of the pores of the bags forms the mortar joints (picture 5.4).

## METHODS OF CONSTRUCTION:

The most popular method is the staging system, though all the methods adopted in the case of the mound could be made use of with additional lifting devices, on proper floating arrangements.

*Staging system:* It consists in erecting on either side a regular staging on piles, bridged over at intervals by braced cross girders. The staging carries over head moving gantries, with tracks for trucks to carry huge concrete blocks of construction. The blocks are bodily lifted and placed in position, with due regard to joints, on a previously prepared firm foundation. The blocks are sometimes shaped to form a "dovetail masonry" in plan (picture 5.2). Heavy Joggles are formed to prevent lateral movements of blocks under the impact of waves. Picture 5.5 shows the method of construction by this method.

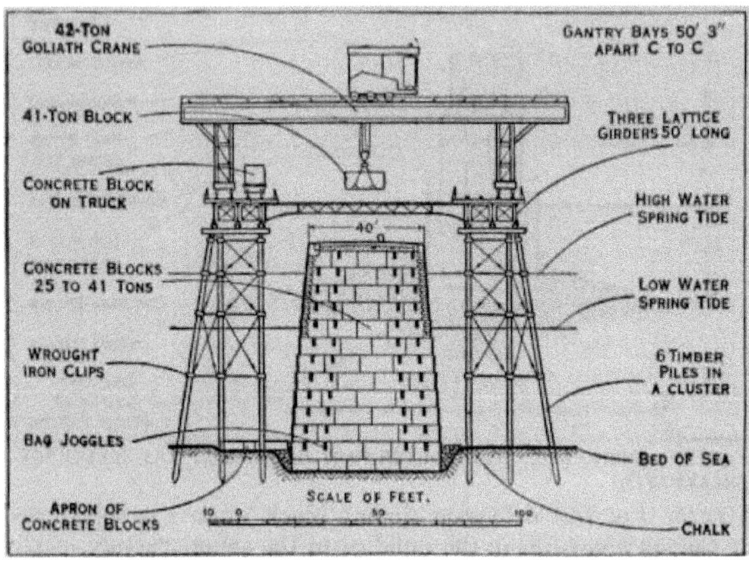


Picture 5.5 Cross-section of staging showing construction of wall breakwater

**Bond:** The blocks have to be properly bonded together and at the same time allow relative settlement, but stop lateral movement. Joggle or Dowel joints as in masonry could be adopted.

# 6. Docks

Docks are enclosed areas for berthing ships, to keep them afloat at a uniform level, to facilitate loading and unloading cargo.

Harbours are prone to be affected by tides, which may cause changes in the water level. If at low tides the level is sufficient as not to ground the ships, the ships could be berthed in these areas.

Thus, in ports on the open sea coast protected by an outlying breakwater, basins are formed within its shelter picture 6.1. In these basins, quay walls are projected at right angles to the shore alongside which vessels can lie and discharge their cargoes.

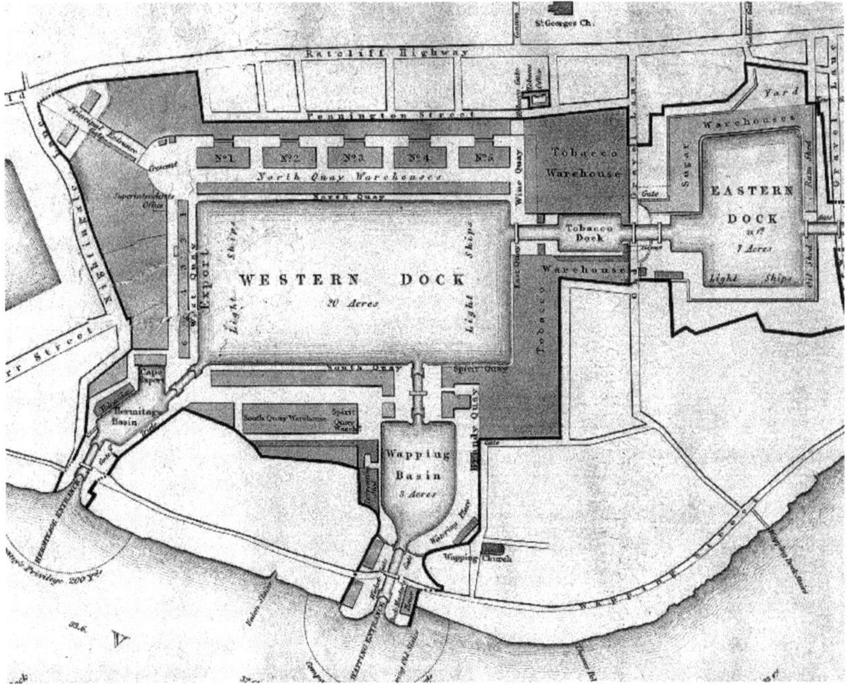

Picture 6.1 Dock Location and Basin formation for London dock Henry Palmer in 1831

## History

The earliest known docks were those discovered in Wadi Al-Jarf, an ancient Egyptian harbor, of Pharaoh Khufu, dating from c.2500 BC located on the Red Sea coast. Archaeologists also discovered anchors and storage jars near the site.

A dock from Lothal in India dates from 2400 BC and was located away from the main current to avoid deposition of silt. Modern oceanographers have observed that the ancient Harappans must have possessed great knowledge relating to tides in order to build such a dock on the ever-shifting course of the Sabarmati, as well as exemplary hydrography and maritime engineering. This is the earliest known dock found in the world equipped to berth and service ships.

It is speculated that Lothal engineers studied tidal movements and their effects on brick-built structures, since the walls are of kiln-burnt bricks. This knowledge also enabled them to select Lothal's location in the first place, as the Gulf of Khambhat has the highest tidal amplitude and ships can be sluiced through flow tides in the river estuary. The engineers built a trapezoidal structure, with north–south arms of average 21.8 meters (71.5 ft), and east–west arms of 37 meters (121 ft).

## British English

In British English, a dock is an enclosed area of water used for loading, unloading, building or repairing ships. Such a dock may be created by building enclosing harbour walls into an existing natural water space, or by excavation within what would otherwise be dry land.

*There are specific types of dock structures where the water level is controlled:*

A wet dock or impounded dock is a variant in which the water is impounded either by dock gates or by a lock, thus allowing ships to remain afloat at low tide in places with high tidal ranges. The level of water in the dock is maintained despite the rising and falling of the tide. This makes transfer of cargo easier. It works like a lock which controls the water level and allows passage of ships. The world's first enclosed wet dock with lock gates to maintain a constant water level irrespective of tidal conditions was the Howland Great Dock on the River Thames, built in 1703. The dock was merely a haven surrounded by trees, with no unloading facilities. The world's first commercial enclosed wet dock, with quays and unloading warehouses, was the Old Dock at Liverpool, built in 1715 and held up to 100 ships. The dock reduced ship waiting giving quick turnarounds, greatly improving the throughput of cargo.

A drydock is another variant, also with dock gates, which can be emptied of water to allow investigation and maintenance of the underwater parts of ships.

A floating dry dock (sometimes just floating dock) is a submersible structure which lifts ships out of the water to allow dry docking where no land-based facilities are available.

*Where the water level is not controlled berths may be:*

Floating, where there is always sufficient water to float the ship.

**NAABSA** (Not Always Afloat but Safely Aground) where ships settle on the bottom at low tide. Ships using NAABSA facilities have to be designed for them.

A dockyard (or shipyard) consists of one or more docks, usually with other structures.

**Open berths:** Where tidal ranges are very marked and large, docks are formed by enclosures. The water level in these enclosures should be maintained at constant level by providing locks and gates.

*Docks* or wet docks are enclosed and are shut off by entrances or locks to maintain a fairly uniform level of water, and basins are partially enclosed areas of water, which are approached by open entrances and are subject to fluctuations of levels, due to tidal variations. These are also known as tidal basins (e.g. Mediterranean Sea).

The permissible tidal range is about 15'-0".

*Advantages of tidal basins:*

(1) Vessels can come in and berth or leave at all times.

(2) Costly arrangements like lock gates are not required.

*Advantages of wet docks:*

(1) Uniform level of water is maintained which is very convenient ' for handling cargo.

(2) Prevents the rubbing of the ships' sides against the quay walls.

(3) Effect of storms in the outer sea and harbour do not obstruct the dock enclosure.

*River ports:* are formed with quays alongside the river banks, where the tidal effect is small. The river in this case serves as the basin (picture 6.2).

When tide ranges are large in such river's, wet docks are constructed, with locks and entrances, which retain the water level during the fall of level in the river.

*Form and arrangements of basins and docks:*

The exact arrangement and form must depend upon the available site. The object to be aimed at in the design is to obtain the maximum length of quay in proportion to the water area of the basin or dock.

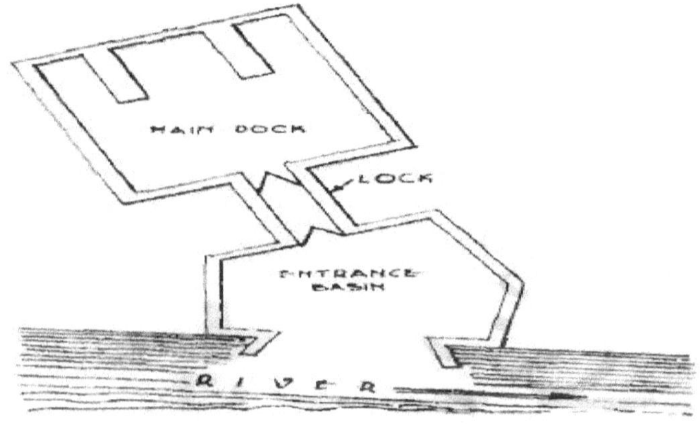


Picture 6.2 Dock Location on River Side

Shape of decks and basins: Should be of shapes formed by straight lines, as curved lines arcs are not suitable for ships to stand alongside.

(i) *Rectangular shape:* The length and breadth could be adjusted to give the maximum quayage (picture 6.3).

Picture 6.3 Basin with protective breakwater

(ii) *Diamond shape:* For the same perpendicular distance between the long sides, the long sides could be conveniently extended (picture 6.4).

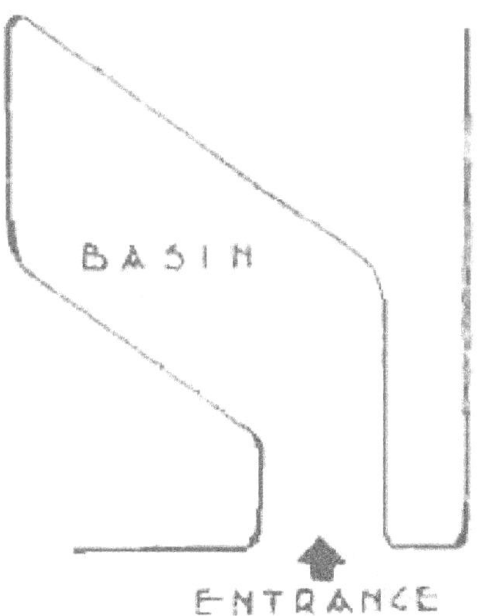


Picture 6.4 Diamond Shaped Harbour

(iii) *Inclined quays type:* It consists of a number of projecting quays into the basin or dock (picture 6.5).

Picture 6.5 Basin with inclined Quays

**Location:** Docks could be located, on inland ports of rivers, at estuaries or on open sea coast. A site on the sea coast is preferable to one up a river as at Kolkata, where navigation of the Hugli River is difficult especially as the river is congested with local traffic. A proper piloting service is necessary for this purpose. The river approach to the dock has to be maintained.

A site on the estuary of a river, if sheltered, broad and free from storms is very good.

**Internal arraignment:** Separate docks are usually required for different kinds of cargo, as for example, coal and oil should be dealt with separately, away from general or food cargo. Flour acquires the smell of its surroundings and should not be discharged near cargo, with strong odour like salted fish.

**Other aspects:**

(1) Availability of fresh water to replace leakage and fouled water from docks. In inland ports separate canal from the rivers will have to be drawn for this purpose, if alternate sources of supply are not available. In the case

of sea coast docks the sea water could be used for cleaning and replenishing the dock.

(2) Approaches must be sheltered and of sufficient depth. In many cases both on the open sea coast or in inland docks, the approach channel has to frequently dredged (picture 6.1).

In certain ports, docks could be approached only at high tides as the approach channel cannot be navigated at low tides.

**Design and construction of basin or dock walls:**

*Design loads:*

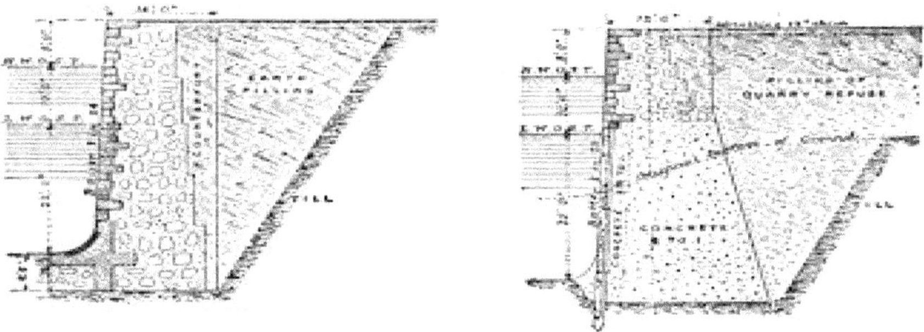

Picture 6.6 Typical section of a dock wall

These walls are designed as gravity retaining wall sections. It should satisfy the following conditions:

(1) Dock empty to withstand pressure of back fill.

(2) Dock full with back fill removed.

(3) Thickness at top should be sufficient to resist the shock of contact with ships.

(4) Dock walls have to carry additional concentrated loads like crane foundations, and capstans or bollard fixtures for mooring ships.

(5) Surcharge loads in the shape of loaded vehicles or trains on the quay adjacent to the wall (picture 6.6).

*Other aspects of construction details:*

(i) Basin walls have to be of much great height than dock walls to allow for the variation in water levels due to tides.

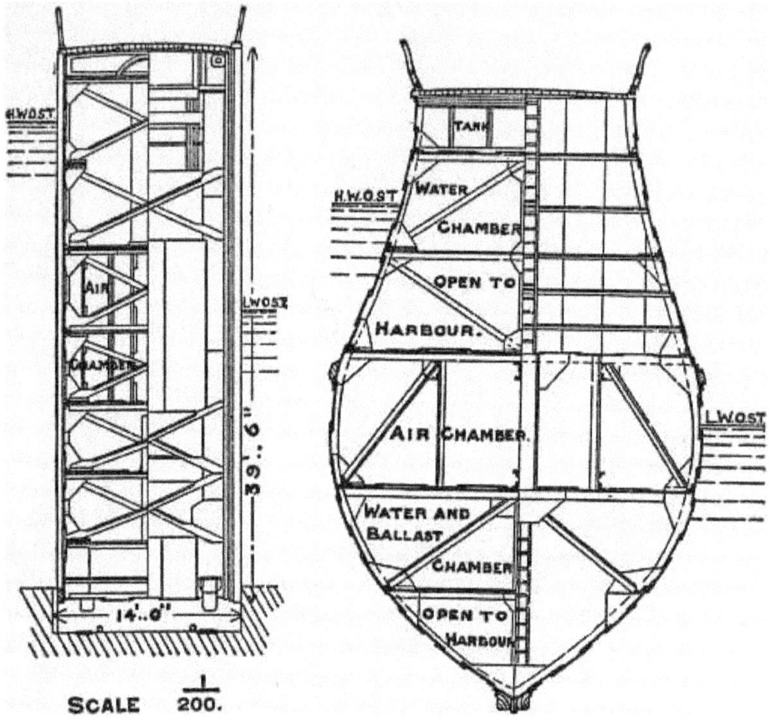


Picture 6.7 (a) Sliding Caisson and (b) Ship Caisson

(ii) As the water level has to be kept constant the sides and bottom should be made impervious and arrangements must be made to supply any loss of water by leakage.

(iii) The front face is generally straight or has a slight batter for ships to stand close to the wall.

(iv) The front face is given a granite fending surface or timber or steel fender to protect the face of the wall from abrasion of ships.

(v) Material for construction: Dock walls are constructed of masonry, brickwork or concrete or a combination of these materials (with construction joints as in the case of concrete walls).

Dock entrances: Docks are entered either directly or through locks. In either case gates are provided for the dock entrances. The types of gates used are:

(1) Wooden or Iron gates as are adopted for locks.

(2) Caissons.

The former type is described in detail under lock gates.

Caissons for dock entrances: Two kinds of caissons are employed:

(1) Sliding caisson.

(2) Ship caisson.

Sliding caisson: It consist of a box shaped steel structure stiffened internally with proper bracing.

It is provided with steel keels sliding on smooth granite floor. Instead of the keels, the caissons could be moved on rollers and rails. The entrance is opened by hauling the caisson into a recess provided in the side of the dock. The caisson also serves as a bridge across the dock entrance.

Ship caisson: Resembles the outline of a ship in cross-section and is constructed of steel with stiffeners at proper intervals. It is floated into position and sunk into specially prepared grooves in the dock sides and sill. The sinking and raising of this caisson is done by ballasting and un-ballasting respectively.

This type does not require any gate recess or machinery for moving (picture 6.7b).

**Sizes of dock entrances:** The width of entrances depends on the largest ship the dock has to receive. Modern ships have beam widths up to 100' nearly, and to accommodate the largest ship the entrance will have to be sufficiently wide for this purpose.

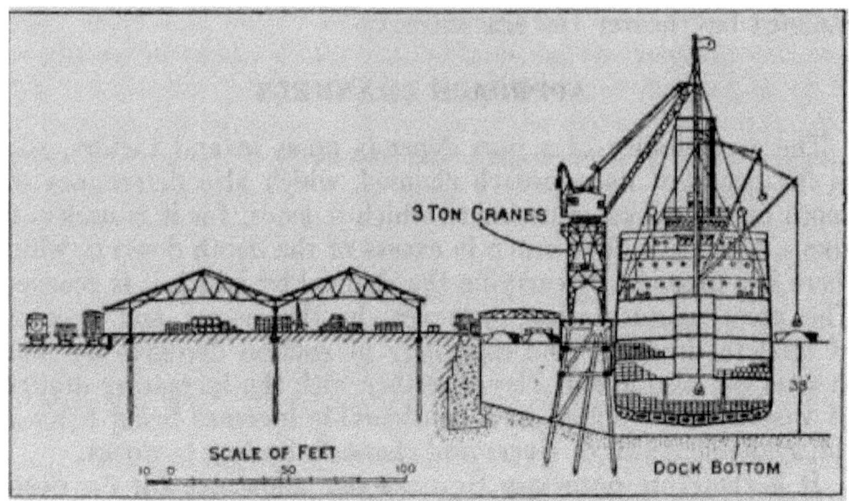


Picture 6.8 Cross section of South Quay and Island jetties of King George V, dock, London. Opened in 1921.

Picture 6.8 illustrates a typical dock and other appurtenances like crane, sheds etc. in the proximate.

# 7. Repair Docks

Repair docks are necessary for the execution of repairs, cleaning and painting of ships' bottom. Hence these docks and docking arrangements should be such as to expose, the ship's exterior fully and keep it out of water during the progress of repairs or renovation. There are generally four classes of such docks viz:

1. Graving or dry dock.

2. Floating dock.

3. Marine railway.

4. Lift docks.

Graving or Dry dock: The graving dock, also known as a dry dock is a long, excavated chamber, having side walls, a semicircular end wall and a floor. The open end of the chamber is provided with a gate and acts as the entrance to the dock. Figs. 7.1 (a) and (b) show the plan and an enlarged cross-section of a typical graving dock.

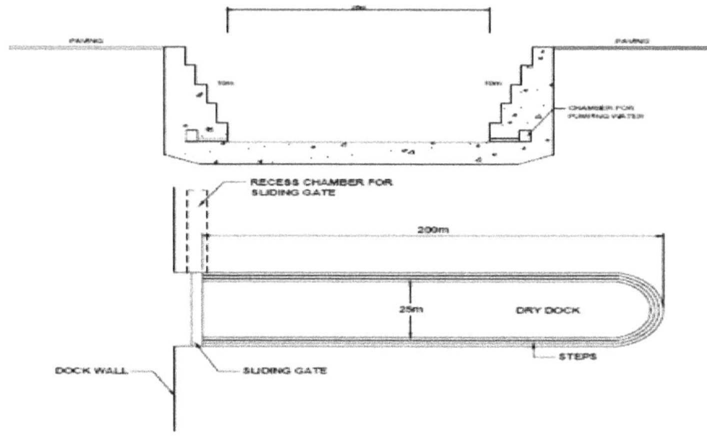


Picture 7.1 (a) Dry Dock Plan

The side walls are formed with a series of steps known as altar courses to receive the ends of the shores which support the vessel in a vertical position while being docked. The dock is constructed of concrete or masonry and the altar courses and steps are of granite to withstand heavy wear. Suitable culverts are also provided in the side walls for filling and emptying the dock.

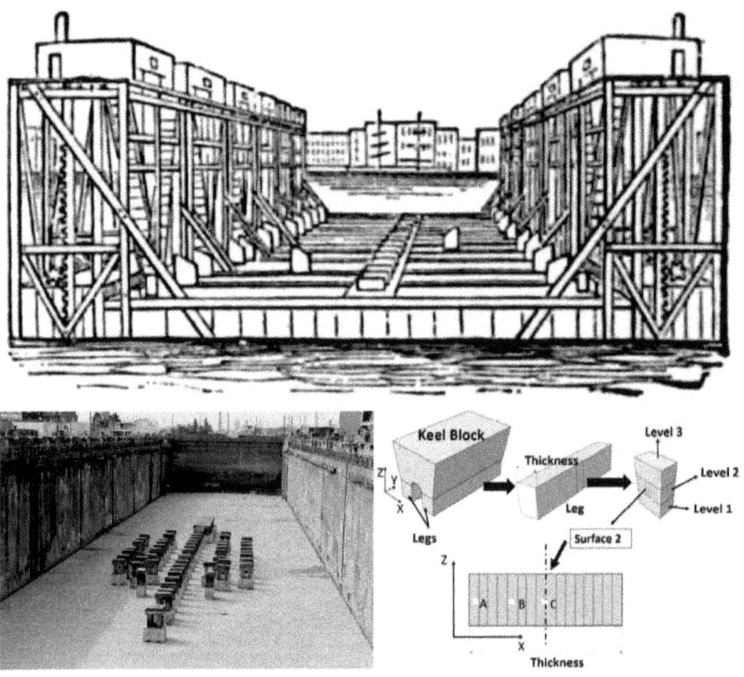


Picture 7.1(b) Enlarged cross section (top), Keel Blocks (bottom)

The dock floor is finished in concrete and is very heavy. On the floor are fixed the keel and bilge blocks on which the ship is brought to rest on the emptying of the dock. The floor has a cross fall to the side, drains which have a longitudinal slope to carry away all wash water. The drains are' protected with proper gratings on top to exclude solids and scrapings carried by the wash, while cleaning the ship's bottom.

Other accessories include big capacity pumps, lifting and hoisting machinery and repair equipment's all suitably housed either on top of, or inside the side walls.

**Method of Dry docking:** The ship enters the dock on adjusting the water level inside the dock to that outside when the entrance gate is closed. The water inside the dock is now pumped out by powerful pumps, the ship being kept vertical and central by the shores between the ship's sides and alter steps while slowly being lowered on to the keel and bilge blocks on which it comes to rest.

**Size of dock:** The size of a dock depends on the size of the largest ship it has to dry dock. Dry docks to handle modern big ships have to be 2,000 ft. in length, with an entrance width of 800 ft. to 1000 ft. The ratio of length to breadth of modern ocean liners are about 9·5 to 1. One of the world's biggest dry docks is built in Shanghai, China. (DATA to be checked and verified. The Esquimalt dry dock has a length of 1150 ft. and breadth of 135 ft. It is constructed of concrete, with granite altars. The pumping plant consists of 3 pumps of 60,000 gallons per minute capacity each, which empties the dock in 4 hours. This would give an idea of the enormity of the dock size as well as its pumping equipment.)

**Forces on a graving dock:** The principal forces to which the dock is subjected are:

1. Weight of ship resting along the center line of dock floor, when dock is empty.

2. Weight of water on the floor when dock is flooded.

3. Upward pressure under the floor when it is being emptied.

4. Earth and hydrostatic pressures behind the side walls.

5. Load imposed by the shores on the inside face of the side walls.

6. Surcharge on the side walls due to cranes and other heavy stationery and moving appliances.

7. In addition to this if there is a strong breeze blowing during dry docking operations, the shores on the leeward side of the ship will be subjected to wind stresses.

For purposes of design the following conditions of loading are to be investigated.

**Dock empty:** The floor is subjected to heavy uplift, which will be considerably more than the weight of the floor itself. This unbalanced excess load is transmitted to the side walls, by "actual" or "virtual" inverted arch action, and being resisted by the weight of the side wall and the horizontal pressures behind it (picture 7.2).

The weight of a ship resting on the empty dock floor, adds concentrated loads along the center line of the floor. Heavy reinforced floor sections may become necessary if the soil is soft or yielding, as intensity of this load may reach as high as 75 tons to 90 tons per running foot. It is generally assumed that 5/8 of such loads are borne by the keel block and 3/8 equally divided on the bilge blocks on either side, at the loaded sections.

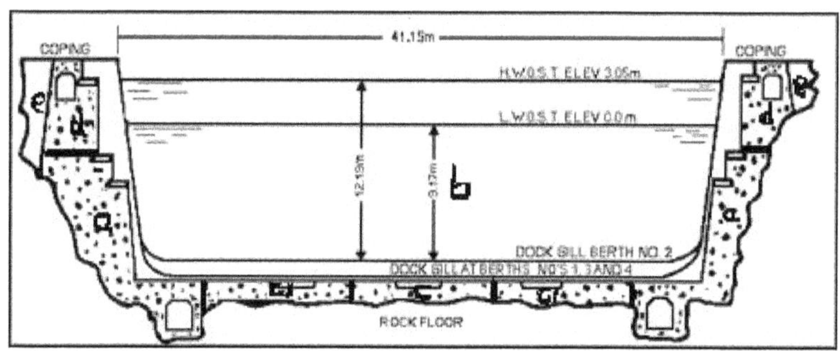


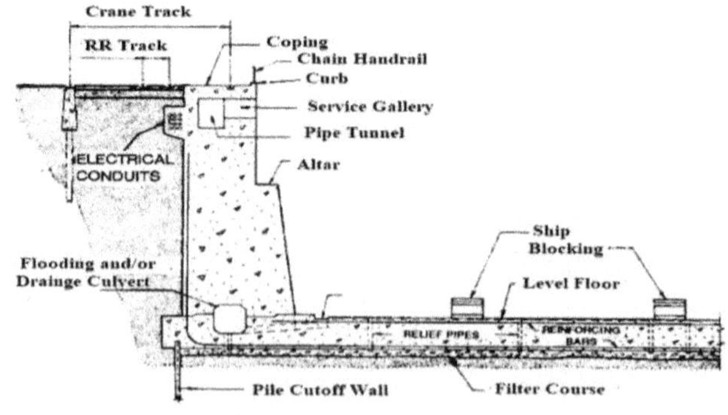


Picture 7.2 Scheme of Dry Dock Construction

**Dock filled with water:** This condition imposes the greatest load on the foundation. The horizontal pressures behind the side wall are more or less resisted by the water pressure inside the dock. The inverted arch action of the floor will be absent under this condition of loading, and the full weight of the side wall less loss due to buoyancy along with the surcharge loads, will have to be taken directly by the foundation.

Scheme of constructing dry docks: Very careful thought has to be bestowed on the effects of horizontal earth and hydrostatic pressures as well as uplift pressures during the construction of docks. The sequence of construction should be so manipulated as to ensure the stability of the structure during construction. The following scheme in this respect is noteworthy: (picture 7.2).

(i) Site is partly excavated and portion marked *a* of the side wall is built.

(ii) The core b is excavated to lay the floor in short lengths and the outer section c1, c2, are laid, leaving the core in between. By doing so only small lengths of the side wall are exposed to the lateral soil and hydrostatic pressure; this pressure being also sustained by the unexcavated central core c of the floor and the completed sections of the floor c1, c2.

(iii) The flooring in the central section is placed after excavating the core c.

(iv) The upper portion of the side wall marked d are constructed.

(v) The back fill e is placed to complete the work.

Design of dry dock floor: The floor of the dry dock sustains loads both from above and below under critical conditions like that of the floor of locks, and floor thickness has to be carefully designed. A simple numerical example will make this aspect very clear. Let us consider the concrete floor of a dry dock to sustain 40 ft. of water over an entrance width of 70 ft. Assuming a modulus of rupture of 10 tons per sq. ft. for cement concrete, a floor thickness of nearly 20 ft. will become necessary, if the foundation below the floor sinks and the concrete slab breaks, in consequence. But actually, such an extreme condition is rare. Then consider the same floor to withstand the upward pressure when the dock is empty, causing a reversal of the original conditions. Of course, this upward pressure is to be taken up by the virtual inverted arch or actual constructed flat arch of the floor. In practice it has been found quite sufficient to design the floor thickness, to accommodate an inverted arch of about 6 ft. thickness and 1/4 rise, adding up to an actual floor thickness of 16 ft. to satisfy all the afore-mentioned conditions.

It would also be necessary to construct the side wall and the floor as independent sections considering the divergent effect of the forces on them. It could be also noticed that constructing the floor slab in sections aids in its action as an inverted flat arch to resist the upward pressure.

Keel and Bilge blocks: Keel block consists of hard wood blocks of very large dimensions. A number of blocks are so spaced along the center line of the dry dock floor, to afford sufficient bearing to the ship's keel, without the blocks being crushed. A typical simple keel block of wood is shown in picture 36. The block is made up of 2 or 3 blocks placed one above the other and is placed at 4 ft. centers longitudinally. The height of the block is about 4 ft. to 4.5 ft., to give enough clearance for workmen to work under the ship [picture 7.1(b)].

Bilge blocks also consist of two or more thicknesses of timber and are fixed on both sides of the 'keel blocks, but at longer intervals apart. The upper part of a bilge block is slightly wedge shaped, for being adjusted under the ship to give a level seating.

Floating dry docks: Floating dock may be defined as "a floating vessel which can lift a ship out of water and retain it above water by means of its own buoyancy". It is a hollow structure of steel, or concrete consisting of 2 side walls and a floor, with the ends open. To receive a ship, the structure is sunk to required depth by ballasting its interior chambers with water, the ship is then floated into position and berthed; the dock is raised bodily with the berthed ship by un-ballasting the chambers by pumping out the water.

Types of floating docks: There are three important types that have been developed viz:

(i) Rigid type or non-self-docking.

(ii) Self docking type.

(iii) Self docking offshore type.

Rigid type: In this type the side walls are rigidly fixed to the pontoon or bottom section (picture7.3). The floor portion is divided into a number of chambers, so as to assist in canting the dock if necessary to berth listing ships, by partial un-ballasting of the chamber.

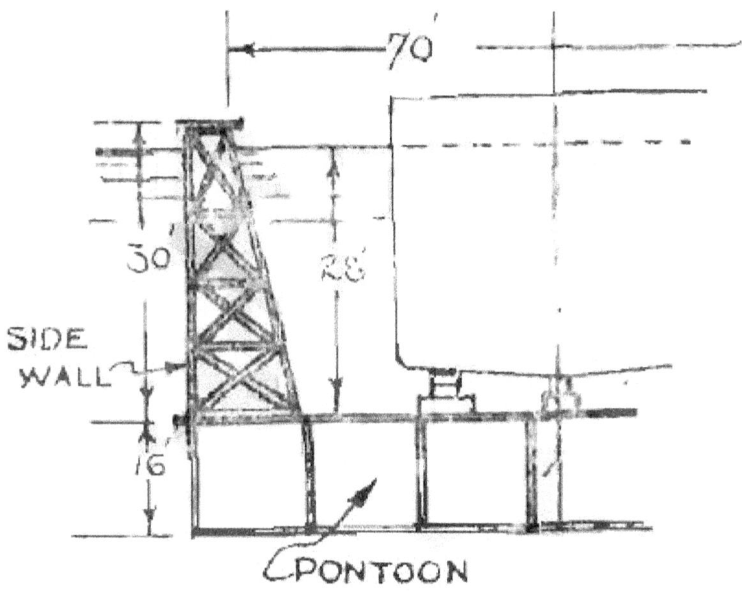


Picture 7.3 Rigid Type Floating Dock

Self-docking type: "Self-docking" refers to a type of floating dock, which is divided into sections longitudinally, anyone of which is capable of being lifted and docked on the remainder of the dock for purposes of, cleaning, painting or repairing. A typical self-docking dry dock, known as Bolted Sectional type is illustrated in picture 7.4; firstly, the whole dock (which is in three sections) is shown assembled; secondly the center section is shown detached and about to be docked on the two end sections; and thirdly an end section is seen being docked on the other two.

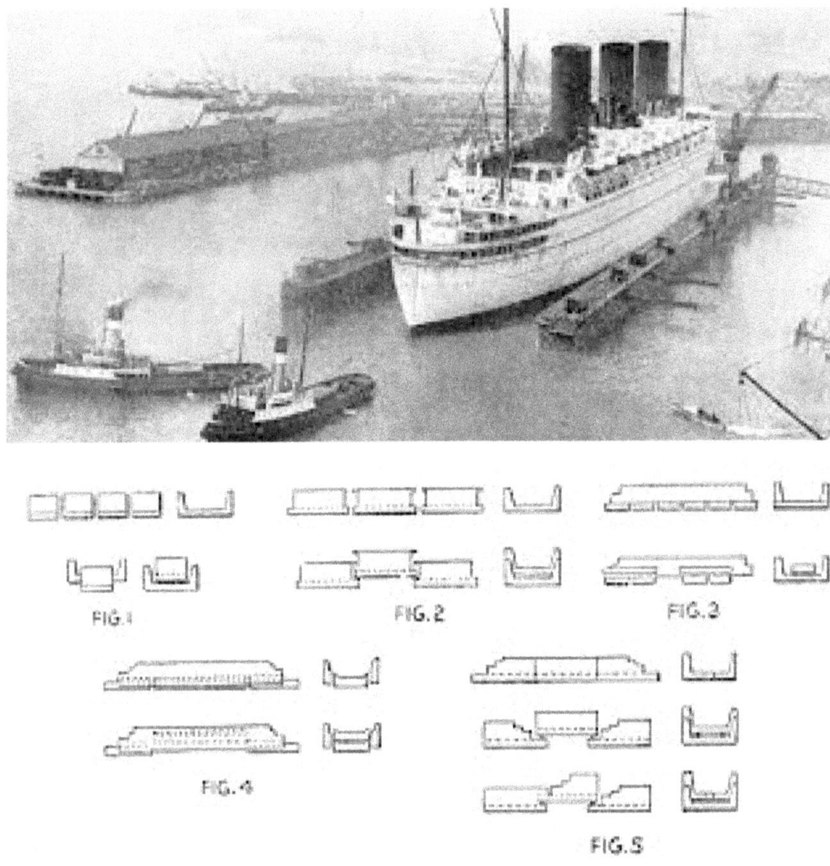


Picture 7.4 Bolted Sectional Floating Dock

This type is usually constructed in" three equal sections, the two end sections having stepped ends to form landings during self-docking. It combines the advantage of strength of the rigid type with self-docking facility.

**The Offshore type:** The offshore dock has no side wall on the water side and has an 'L' shaped cross-section. The side wall is connected to the shore by hinged parallel booms capable of lifting or lowering the dock. The ship to be docked, could be brought on to the dock from either end or sideways. The dock is longitudinally made into two sections, so as to dock one half on the other. The dock and the self-docking operation is illustrated in picture 7.5. This type of dock is convenient in a sheltered situation and adaptable for being attached to river quays.

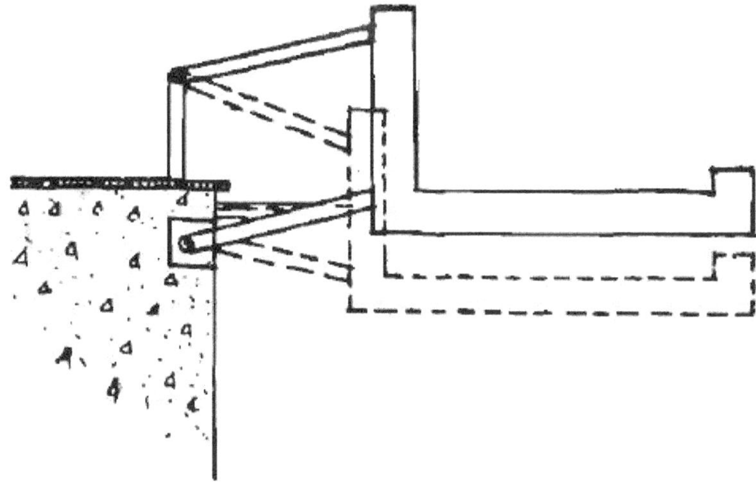

Picture 7.5 Offshore Dock (Self Docking)

**Design considerations:** The design of floating docks has to be considered in respect of two conditions, viz:

(i) *When loaded with a ship:* The transverse strength of the structure should be sufficient to enable the buoyancy of the side walls and the side sections of the pontoon to carry the concentrated load of the ship along the longitudinal central axis of the floor.

(ii) *When unloaded and floating:* The transverse strength should be sufficient to support the weight of the side walls and other heavy machinery carried by or on the side walls, like pumping units, cranes, etc.

When a ship is on the dock, and the dock commences to rise, the water ballast from the side walls is unballasted first. The sheath or skin of the side walls will thus be exposed to the outside water pressure and has to withstand this pressure. The maximum pressure will be attained, when the side wall is fully empty and the dock is still immersed and in the process of rising. In most floating docks this pressure is not allowed to exceed 20 ft. head of water. In order to get the full lifting effect a floating dry dock has to be fully unballasted which results in the dock structure taking all the transverse bending strain. A correct manipulation of the pumping out of ballast will ensure avoidance of any undue or excessive strain on the structure.

*Advantages of floating dry dock:*

(i) It is cheaper in initial and working cost.

(ii) It could be constructed in half the time it takes to construct a graving dock of the same capacity.

(iii) It has the advantage of mobility and could be transferred from port to port.

(iv) It could be trimmed to take a damaged and listing ship, which are not possible to tow through the entrance of a graving dock.

(v) It has no elaborate entrance or gate arrangements.

*Disadvantages of floating dry docks:*

(i) The durability or service life is appreciably less. The floating dock being a steel structure constantly afloat in sea water could have a life of only about 50 years, like any other steel structure, whereas a well-constructed graving dock is practically indestructible.

(ii) Upkeep and maintenance are more since a floating dry dock itself is a large floating vessel and needs dry docking, cleaning, painting etc.

(iii) The maneuvering and towing of a floating dry dock needs great skill and care and in exposed situations it may not be possible to use it at all.

**Marine railway:** Marine railway is an inclined railway extending from the shore well into the water as well as the foreshore, to enable a ship to be drawn up clear out of the water. The essential parts are cradle, which moves up and down an inclined track and the track itself supported on an unyielding and firm foundation or pile foundations.

The cradle or platform (picture 7.6) is constructed of steel and provided with keel and bilge blocks to receive the ship.

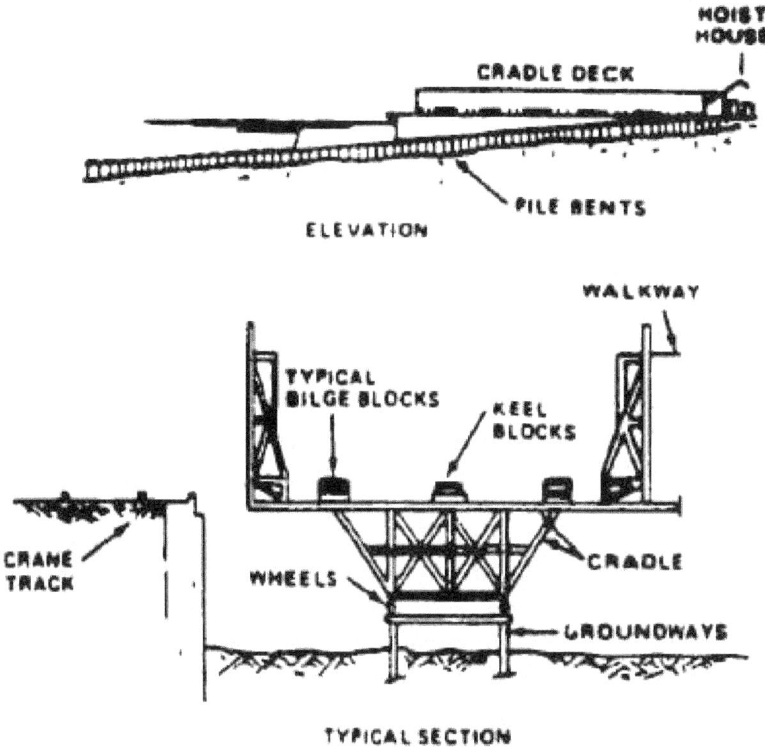


Fig 7.6 Cradle Deck

The cradle is mounted on a system of rollers which move on iron tracks carried by longitudinal timbers, supported on cross ties or beams bearing on piles or other firm foundations. Strong cables attached to the shore end of the cradle haul the cradle, operated by strong mechanical winches built on shore.

The ways consist of heavy rails secured to longitudinal sleepers supported on cross ties, and laid at an inclination varying from 1 in 15 to 1 in 20. A rocking device to receive the safety pawls under the cradle is placed in the center of the ways, to keep the cradle from slipping back if the hauling cable breaks.

For dry docking the cradle is slipped down into deep water and the ship to be docked is towed over the cradle and positioned to rest and moored to the towers on either side of the cradle. The cradle slowly emerges above the H. Water level, when hauled up the ways, permitting the ship to come to rest, on the cradle floor as the cable reaches the normal docking position.

The use of this type of dock is no doubt economical but is limited to vessels of not more than 5000 tons. In modern naval practice this type is yielding place to graving docks and floating docks which have become popular.

**Lift dry dock:** These are substantially constructed platforms capable of being lowered into and raised from water. Raising and lowering is accomplished by means of hydraulic power applied through cylinders supporting the ends of cross girders carrying the platform. As modern ships have considerably grown in tonnage and size, this ancient method of dry docking had to be discontinued, giving way to more efficient and less cumbersome types.

**Auxiliary repair dock**

An auxiliary repair dock (ARD) is a type of floating drydock employed by the U.S. Navy, especially during World War II. The Navy commissioned 33 ARD vessels: ARD-1 through ARD-33. ARDs were self-sustaining in World War II. ARDs have a rudder to help in tow moving, making ARDs very mobile, and have a bow to cut through waves. ARDs have a stern that can be opened or closed. The stern can be closed with bottom-hinged flap gate, operated by hydraulic rams. This stern gate can be lowered for ship entrance into the submerged dock, and then closed to keep out waves. ARDs were built by the Pacific Bridge Company, in Alameda, California.

*Primary use*

The Auxiliary repair dock was a type of Auxiliary floating drydock, which could, by design, provide drydock facilities to damaged Navy vessels. Floating drydocks of this type were approximately 500-foot (150 m) long and weighted about 5,000 tons. The first auxiliary repair dock was the USS ARD-1, built by the Pacific Bridge Company and completed in September 1934. ARD-1 was 393 feet and 6 inches (119.94 m) long, and could lift 2200 tons. ARD-1 was so successful that 30 ARDs were built, most completed between 1942 and 1944. ARD-2 and the next five ARD docks were larger at 3500 tons. and 485'8" (148.0m) long. ARD-1 was taken to a forward Naval base at Kerama Retto, Okinawa Island, to repair the many ships damaged by kamikaze attacks. ARD-1 made many temporary repairs to get ships back into action. Many other ARDs joined ARD-1 in this important task. This minimized the time ships were out of action for repairs.

*Drydock facility*

Floating drydocks, both ARDs and some other types, are capable of flooding themselves to partially submerge underwater, opening up a bow door to permit a damaged vessel to enter. Once the damaged vessel was above the floating drydock, the door was closed and water was pumped out of the floating drydock, permitting repair work to be performed on the damaged vessel. Such work in battle areas was often of a temporary nature, primarily to return the damaged vessel to seaworthy condition.

Once the damaged vessel was sufficiently repaired, the floating drydock was flooded, the door opened, and the repaired vessel allowed to depart for further duty or assignment.

*Personnel capabilities*

While the damaged vessel was being repaired, the drydock was capable of providing the crew of the damaged ship with temporary necessities, such as meals, laundry, some supplies, and, in a limited number of cases, berthing for crew members. (When possible, the crew of the damaged ship remained on their ship while structural repair was being accomplished.)

Picture 7.7 Auxiliary repair dock

# 8. Entrance Locks

Locks giving access to docks resemble in Principle River or canal locks.

The lock consists of a chamber, enclosed by quay walls on each side and is *paved at the bottom by an inverted arc* flooring, to resist the upward water pressure, when the lock level is low. This floor abuts against the side walls, protecting them against sliding due to earth pressure when lock is empty or has a low level of water. The gates closing the entrance are constructed of wood or iron of heavy design to stand heavy water pressure. These gates close against a sill provided for the purpose. The sill is raised above the gate floor by 2'.

Sluice ways are formed in the side walls for filling and emptying locks (picture 8.1).

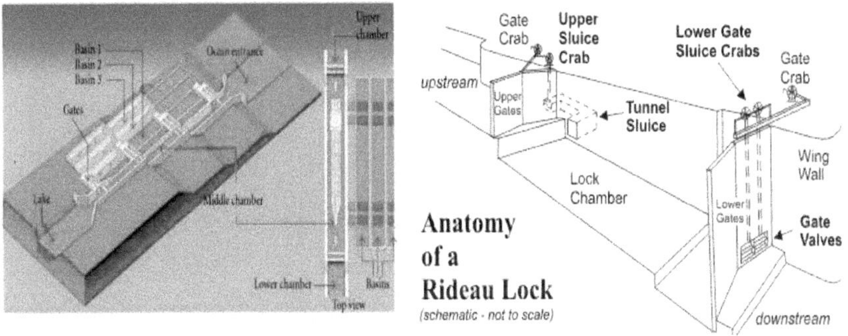


Picture 8.1 Plan of Lock

**Lock foundations:** Foundations have to be carried with special care, so as to secure the lock against settlement. Foundations generally adopted are,

(a) On bearing piles protected by sheet piles around, or

(b) On hard pan.

**Dimensions of entrances and locks:** Depend on the width, Size and displacement of the longest vessel using the lock and dock. Modern locks have widths varying from 80' and above and depth 25' to 40' and lengths of 800' and over. Picture 8.2 shows a typical lock, with an enlarged plan showing the details of the gate floor.

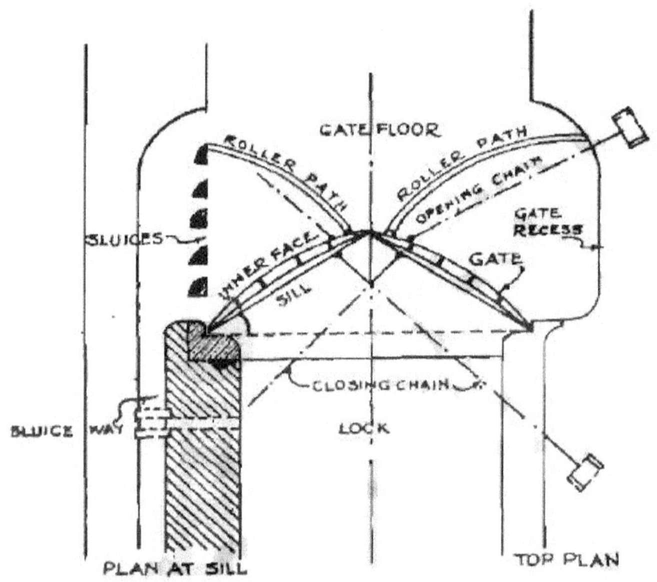


Picture 8.2 (a) Plan of floor gate

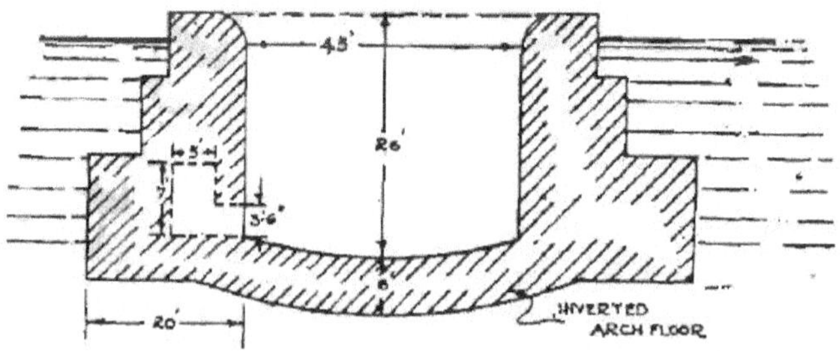


Picture 8.2 (b) Cross-section of Lock

**Pound lock**

A pound lock is a type of lock that is used almost exclusively nowadays on canals and rivers. A pound lock has a chamber with gates at both ends that control the level of water in the pound. In contrast, an earlier design with a single gate was known as a flash lock.

Pound locks were first used in China during the Song Dynasty (960–1279 AD), having been pioneered by the Song politician and naval engineer Qiao Weiyue in 984. They replaced earlier double slipways that had caused trouble and are mentioned by the Chinese polymath Shen Kuo (1031–1095) in his book Dream Pool Essays (published in 1088), and fully described in the Chinese historical text Song Shi (compiled in 1345).

The distance between the two locks was rather more than 50 paces, and the whole space was covered with a great roof like a shed. The gates were 'hanging gates'; when they were closed the water accumulated like a tide until the required level was reached, and then when the time came it was allowed to flow out.

The water level could differ by 4 feet (1.2 m) or 5 feet (1.5 m) at each lock and in the Grand Canal the level was raised in this way by 138 feet (42 m).

In medieval Europe a sort of pound lock was built in 1373 at Vreeswijk, Netherlands. This pound lock serviced many ships at once in a large basin. Yet the first true pound lock was built in 1396 at Damme near Bruges, Belgium. The Italian Bertola da Novate (c. 1410–1475) constructed 18-pound locks on the Naviglio di Bereguardo (part of the Milan canal system sponsored by Francesco Sforza) between 1452 and 1458.

Picture 8.3 A Pound lock on the Keitele–Päijänne Canal at Äänekoski in Central Finland

**Use in river navigation**

When a stretch of river is made navigable, a lock is sometimes required to bypass an obstruction such as a rapid, dam, or mill weir – because of the change in river level across the obstacle.

In large scale river navigation improvements, weirs and locks are used together. A weir will increase the depth of a shallow stretch, and the required lock will either be built in a gap in the weir, or at the downstream end of an artificial cut which bypasses the weir and perhaps a shallow stretch of river below it. A river improved by these means is often called a Waterway or River Navigation.

Sometimes a river is made entirely non-tidal by constructing a sea lock directly into the estuary.

In more advanced river navigations, more locks are required.

Where a longer cut bypasses a circuitous stretch of river, the upstream end of the cut will often be protected by a flood lock.

The longer the cut, the greater the difference in river level between start and end of the cut, so that a very long cut will need additional locks along its length. At this point, the cut is, in effect, a canal.

Picture 8.4 Locks on the Rideau Canal, Entrance Valley, near Parliament Hill, Ottawa, Canada

**Use in canals**

Early completely artificial canals, across fairly flat countryside, would get round a small hill or depression by simply detouring (contouring) around it. As engineers became more ambitious in the types of country they felt they could overcome, locks became essential to effect the necessary changes in water level without detours that would be completely uneconomic both in building costs and journey time. Later still, as construction techniques improved, engineers became more willing to cut directly through and across obstacles by constructing long tunnels, cuttings, aqueducts or embankments, or to construct even more technical devices such as inclined planes or boat lifts. However, locks continued to be built to supplement these solutions, and are an essential part of even the most modern navigable waterways.

Picture 8.5 Locks of the Panama Canal during construction

## Basic construction and operation

**All pound locks have three elements:**

A watertight chamber connecting the upper and lower canals, and large enough to enclose one or more boats. The position of the chamber is fixed, but its water level can vary.

A gate (often a pair of "pointing" half-gates) at each end of the chamber. A gate is opened to allow a boat to enter or leave the chamber; when closed, the gate is watertight.

A set of lock gear to empty or fill the chamber as required. This is usually a simple valve (traditionally, a flat panel (paddle) lifted by manually winding a rack and pinion mechanism) which allows water to drain into or out of the chamber; larger locks may use pumps.

The principle of operating a lock is simple. For instance, if a boat travelling downstream finds the lock already full of water:

The entrance gates are opened and the boat moves in.

The entrance gates are closed.

A valve is opened, this lowers the boat by draining water from the chamber.

The exit gates are opened and the boat moves out.

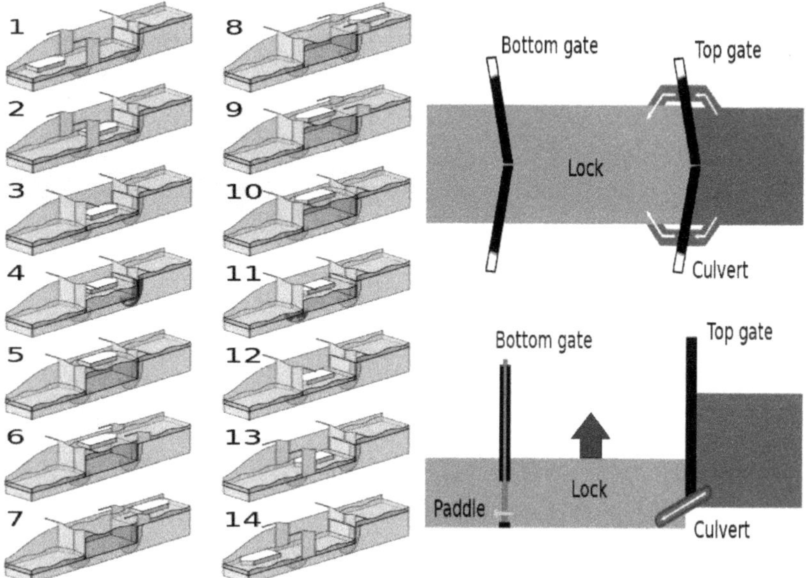


Picture 8.6 (a) Picture 1-7 for boat going upstream and picture 8-14 for boat going downstream (b) A plan and side view of a generic, empty canal lock. A lock chamber separated from the rest of the canal by an upper pair and a lower pair of mitre gates. The gates in each pair close against each other at an 18° angle to approximate an arch against the water pressure on the "upstream" side of the gates when the water level on the "downstream" side is lower.

If the lock were empty, the boat would have had to wait 5 to 10 minutes while the lock was filled. For a boat travelling upstream, the process is reversed; the boat enters the empty lock, and then the chamber is filled by opening a valve that allows water to enter the chamber from the upper level. The whole operation will usually take between 10 and 20 minutes, depending on the size of the lock and whether the water in the lock was originally set at the boat's level.

Boaters approaching a lock are usually pleased to meet another boat coming towards them, because this boat will have just exited the lock on their level and therefore set the lock in their favour – saving about 5 to 10 minutes. However, this is not true for staircase locks, where it is quicker for boats to go through in convoy.

Picture 8.7 Operation of a canal lock, 1–3. Boat enters 'empty' lock, 4. Bottom gates are closed, bottom paddles closed, top paddles opened, lock starts to fill, 5. Lock is filling with water, lifting boat to the higher level

## Details and terminology

For simplicity, this section describes a basic type of lock, with a pair of gates at each end of the chamber and simple rack and pinion paddles raised manually by means of a detachable windlass operated by lock-keepers or the boat's shore crew. This type can be found all over the world, but the terminology here is that used on the British canals. A subsequent section explains common variations.

Picture 8.8 A drained lock chamber

*Rise*

The rise is the change in water-level in the lock. The two deepest locks on the English canal system are Bath deep lock on the Kennet and Avon Canal and Tuel Lane Lock on the Rochdale Canal, which both have a rise of nearly 20 feet (6.1 m). Both locks are amalgamations of two separate locks, which were combined when the canals were restored to accommodate changes in road crossings. The deepest "as-built" locks in England are considered to be Etruria Top Lock on the Trent and Mersey Canal and Somerton Deep Lock on the Oxford Canal: both have a rise of about 14 ft (4.3 m). Again, sources vary as to which is the deepest, and in any case Etruria has been deepened over the years to accommodate subsidence. By comparison, the Carrapatelo and Valeira locks on the Douro River in Portugal, which are 279 feet (85 m) long and 39 feet (12 m) wide, have maximum lifts of 115 feet (35 m) and 108 feet (33 m) respectively. The two Ardnacrusha locks near Limerick on the Shannon navigation in Ireland have a rise of 100 feet (30 m). The upper chamber rises 60 feet (18 m) and is connected to the lower chamber by a tunnel, which when descending does not become visible until the chamber is nearly empty.

*Pound*

A pound is the level stretch of water between two locks (also known as a reach). On American canals, a pound is called a level.

*Chamber*

The chamber is the main feature of a lock. It is a watertight (masonry, brick, steel or concrete) enclosure which can be sealed off from the pounds at both ends by means of gates. The chamber may be the same size (plus a little maneuvering room) as the largest vessel for which the waterway was designed; sometimes larger, to allow more than one such vessel at a time to use the lock. The chamber is said to be "full" when the water level is the same as in the upper pound; and "empty" when the level is the same as in the lower pound. (If the lock has no water in it at all, perhaps for maintenance work, it might also be said to be empty, but it is more usually described as "drained" or "dewatered".)

Picture 8.9 The chamber of the 35 m lock at Carrapatelo Dam in Portugal

*Cill*

The cill, also spelled sill, is a narrow horizontal ledge protruding a short way into the chamber from below the upper gates. Allowing the rear of the boat to "hang" on the cill is the main danger when descending a lock, and the position of the forward edge of the cill is usually marked on the lock side by a white line. The edge of the cill is usually curved, protruding less in the center than at the edges. In some locks, there is a piece of oak about 9 in (23 cm) thick which protects the solid part of the lock cill. On the Oxford Canal it is called a babbie; on the Grand Union Canal it is referred to as the cill bumper. Some canal operation authorities, primarily in the United States and Canada, call the ledge a miter sill (mitre sill in Canada).

*Gates*

Gates are the watertight doors which seal off the chamber from the upper and lower pounds. Each end of the chamber is equipped with a gate, or pair of half-gates, made of oak or elm (or now sometimes steel). The most common arrangement, usually called miter gates, was invented by Leonardo da Vinci sometime around the late 15th century. When closed, a pair meet at an angle like a chevron pointing upstream and only a very small difference in water-level is necessary to squeeze the closed gates securely together. This reduces any leaks from between them and prevents their being opened until water levels have equalized. If the chamber is not full, the top gate is secure; and if the chamber is not completely empty, the bottom gate is secure (in normal operation, therefore, the chamber cannot be open at both ends). A lower gate is taller than an upper gate, because the upper gate only has to be tall enough to close off the upper pound, while the lower gate has to be able to seal off a full chamber. The upper gate is as tall as the canal is deep, plus a little more for the balance beam, winding mechanism, etc.; the lower gate's height equals the upper gate plus the lock's rise.

*Balance beam*

A balance beam is the long arm projecting from the landward side of the gate over the towpath. As well as providing leverage to open and close the heavy gate, the beam also balances the (non-floating) weight of the gate in its socket, and so allows the gate to swing more freely.

*Paddle*

A paddle – sometimes known as a slacker, clough, or (in American English) wicket – is the simple valve by which the lock chamber is filled or emptied. The paddle itself is a sliding wooden (or nowadays plastic) panel which when "lifted" (slid up) out of the way allows water to either enter the chamber from the upper pound or flow out to the lower pound. A gate paddle simply covers a hole in the lower part of a gate; a more sophisticated ground paddle blocks an underground culvert. There can be up to 8 paddles (two gate paddles and two ground paddles at both upper and lower ends of the chamber) but there will often be fewer. For a long period since the 1970s it was British Waterways policy not to provide gate paddles in replacement top gates if two ground paddles existed. The reason for this was given as safety, since it is possible for an ascending boat to be swamped by the water from a carelessly lifted gate paddle. However, without the gate paddles the locks are slower to operate and this has been blamed in some places for causing congestion. Since the late 1990s the preferred method has been to retain or re-install the gate paddles and fit 'baffles' across them to minimize the risk of inundation.

On the old Erie Canal, there was a danger of injury when operating the paddles: water, on reaching a certain position, would push the paddles with a force which could tear the windlass (or handle) out of one's hands, or if one was standing in the wrong place, could knock one into the canal, leading to injuries and drownings.

*Winding gear or paddle gear*

Winding gear is the mechanism which allows paddles to be lifted (opened) or lowered (closed). Typically, a square-section stub emerges from the housing of the winding gear. This is the axle of a sprocket ("pinion") which engages with a toothed bar ("rack") attached by rodding to the top of the paddle. A lock-keeper or member of the boat's shore crew engages the square socket of their windlass (see below) onto the end of the axle and turns the windlass perhaps a dozen times. This rotates the pinion and lifts the paddle. A pawl engages with the rack to prevent the paddle from dropping inadvertently while being raised, and to keep it raised when the windlass is removed, so that the operator can attend to other paddles. Nowadays it is considered discourteous and wasteful of water to leave a paddle open after a boat has left the lock, but in commercial days it was normal practice. To lower a paddle the pawl must be disengaged and the paddle wound down with the windlass. Dropping paddles by knocking the pawl off can cause damage to the mechanism; the paddle gear is typically made of cast iron and can shatter or crack when dropped from a height. In areas where water-wastage due to vandalism is a problem, (for example the Birmingham Canal Navigations), paddle mechanisms are commonly fitted with vandal-proof locks (nowadays rebranded "water conservation devices") which require the boater to employ a key before the paddle can be lifted. The keys are officially known as "water conservation keys", but boaters usually refer to them as T-keys, from their shape; handcuff keys because the original locks, fitted on the Leeds and Liverpool Canal, resembled handcuffs; Leeds and Liverpool Keys after that canal; or simply Anti-Vandal Keys.

*Hydraulic paddle gear*

During the 1980s, British Waterways began to introduce a hydraulic system for operating paddles, especially those on bottom gates, which are the heaviest to operate. A metal cylinder about a foot in diameter was mounted on the balance beam and contained a small oil-operated hydraulic pump. A spindle protruded from the front face and was operated by a windlass in the usual way, the energy being transferred to the actual paddle by small bore pipes. The system was widely installed and, on some canals, it became very common. There turned out to be two serious drawbacks. It was much more expensive to install and maintain than traditional gear and went wrong more frequently, especially once vandals learned to cut the pipes. Even worse, it had a safety defect, in that the paddle once in the raised position could not be dropped in an emergency, but had to be wound down, taking a good deal longer. These factors led to the abandonment of the policy in the late 1990s, but examples of it survive all over the system, as it is usually not removed until the gates need replacing, which happens about every twenty years.

*Windlass ("lock key")*

A windlass (also variously 'lock handle', 'iron' or simply 'key') is a detachable crank used for opening lock paddles (the word does not refer to the winding mechanism itself).

The simplest windlass is made from an iron rod of circular section, about half an inch in diameter and two feet long, bent to make an L-shape with legs of slightly different length. The shorter leg is called the handle, and the longer leg is called the arm. Welded to the end of the arm is a square, sometimes tapered, socket of the correct size to fit onto the spindle protruding from lock winding gear.

- Socket: Traditionally, windlasses had a single socket, designed for a particular canal. When undertaking a journey through several canals with different lock-gear spindle sizes it was necessary to carry several different windlasses. A modern windlass usually has two sockets for use on different canals: the smaller is for the British Waterways standard spindle, fitted in the early 1990s almost everywhere, the larger for the gear on the Grand Union Canal north of Napton Junction, which they were unable/unwilling to convert.

- Handle: The handle is long enough for a two-handed grip and is far enough from the socket to give enough leverage to wind the paddle up or down. There may be a freely rotating sleeve around the handle to protect the hands from the friction of rough iron against skin.

- Arm: A "long throw" windlass has a longer arm so that the handle is further from the socket to give a greater leverage on stiffer paddles. If the throw is too long then the user, winding a gate paddle, risks barking their knuckles against the balance beam when the handle is at the lowest point of its arc. A sophisticated modern windlass may have an adjustable-length arm.

- Materials: Early windlasses were individually hand forged from a single piece of wrought iron by a blacksmith. More modern techniques include casting of iron or bronze, drop forging and (the most common technique) welding. Some boatmen had their windlasses 'silvered' (or chrome plated) for increased comfort and to prevent rusting. Windlasses are now only rarely plated, but a popular modern choice of metal is aluminum, whose smooth and rustproof surface has the same advantages of longevity and blister-reduction, and is also very light. One type of these, the Dunton

Double, has only a single eye, but by clever tapering it will operate either size of spindle.

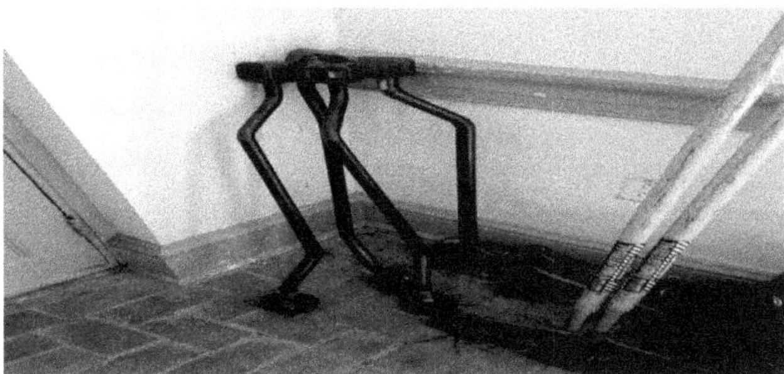

Picture 8.10 Collection of lock windlasses. Note: rakes are for clearing trash out of the lock

On the Chesapeake and Ohio Canal, the lockkeepers were required to remove the windlasses from all lock paddles at night, to prevent unauthorized use.

**Variations**

Variations exist for types of locks and the terminology used for them.

*Single gates*

Single gates are often installed on narrow canals (locks approx. 7 feet or 2.1 meters wide).

On most English narrow canals, the upper end of the chamber is closed by a single gate the full width of the lock. This was cheaper to construct and is quicker to operate with a small crew, as only one gate needs to be opened. These were often fitted with a post allowing a rope to be used to stop the boat and close the gate at the same time.

Some narrow locks (e.g. on Birmingham Canal Navigations) go even further. They have single gates at the lower end also. This speeds up passage, even though single lower gates are heavy (heavier than a single upper gate, because the lower gate is taller) and the lock has to be longer (a lower gate opens INTO the lock, it has to pass the bow or stern of an enclosed boat, and a single gate has a wider arc than two half-gates).

*Steel gates*

Steel gates and/or balance beams are frequently used nowadays, although all-wooden versions are still fitted where appropriate.

- Swinging gates. Even very large steel-gated locks still can use essentially the same swinging gate design as small 250-year-old locks on the English canals. On English canals, steel gates usually have wooden mitre posts as this gives a better seal.
- Sliding gates. Some low-head locks use sliding steel gates (see Kiel Canal). The sliding gates of the Nieuwe Meersluis in Amsterdam double as roadways.
- Caisson gates. A kind of sliding gate that is hollow and can float. It can be constructed to withstand high heads.
- Guillotine gates. Some locks have vertically moving steel gates – these are quite common on river navigations in East Anglia. Sometimes just one of the pairs of swinging gates is replaced by a guillotine: for instance, at Salter Hebble Locks, where space to swing the balance beams of bottom gates of the lowest lock was restricted by bridge widening. On the River Nene most locks have this arrangement as in time of flood the top mitre gates are chained open and the bottom guillotines lifted so that the lock chamber acts as an overflow sluice. Guillotine gates are also used on the downstream side of larger locks such as the 23m Bollène lock on the River Rhône, the aperture being large enough for a boat to travel under it.

Picture 8.11 Example of a lock with a drop gate (Lock 10) on the Chesapeake and Ohio Canal

- Vertically rotating gates (American usage: Drop gates) are gates which, when open, lie flat on the canal bed and which close by lifting (London Flood Barrier). Some of these were installed on the Chesapeake and Ohio Canal in the congested 7 Locks area since they could be operated by one man and also could speed up traffic.
- Rotating-sector gates. Some of these works very like traditional swinging gates, but with each gate in the form of a sector of a cylinder. They close by rotating out from the lock wall and meeting in the center of the chamber. Water is let in or out by opening the gates slightly: there may be no paddles or other lock gear. The lock at Limehouse Basin, which gives access to the River Thames, is an example. A dramatically large one can be seen at the Maeslantkering (huge flood gates) near Rotterdam. There is a different type at the sea lock on the Ribble Link: this is a rising sector gate, which has a horizontal axis: the gate drops to the bed of the river to allow boats to pass.

*Different paddle gear*

Some manually operated paddles do not require a detachable handle (windlass) because they have their handles ready-attached.

On the Leeds and Liverpool Canal there is a variety of different lock gear. Some paddles are raised by turning what is in effect a large horizontal wing nut (butterfly nut) lifting a screw-threaded bar attached to the top of the paddle. Others are operated by lifting a long wooden lever, which operates a wooden plate which seals the culvert. These are known locally as "jack cloughs". Bottom gate paddles are sometimes operated by a horizontal ratchet which also slides a wooden plate sideways, rather than the more common vertical lift. Many of these idiosyncratic paddles have been "modernized" and they are becoming rare.

On the Calder and Hebble Navigation, some paddle gear is operated by repeatedly inserting a Calder and Hebble Handspike (length of 4" by 2" hardwood) into a ground-level slotted wheel and pushing down on the handspike to rotate the wheel on its horizontal axis.

On some parts of the Montgomery Canal bottom paddles are used in place of side paddles. Rather than passing into the lock through a culvert around the side of the lock gate, the water flows through a culvert in the bottom of the canal. The paddle slides horizontally over the culvert.

*Composite locks*

To economies, especially where good stone would be prohibitively expensive or difficult to obtain, composite locks were made, i.e. they were constructed using rubble or inferior stone, dressing the inside walls of the lock with wood, so as not to abrade the boats. This was done, for instance, on the Chesapeake and Ohio Canal with the locks near the Paw Paw Tunnel and also the Chenango Canal, because the wood would swell (making the lock space smaller) or rot away, the wood was often replaced by concrete.

*Lock keepers*

Some locks are operated (or at least supervised) by professional or volunteer lock keepers. This is particularly true on commercial waterways, or where locks are large or have complicated features that the average leisure boater may not be able to operate successfully. For instance, although the Thames above Teddington (England) is almost entirely a leisure waterway, the locks are usually staffed. Only recently have boaters been allowed limited access to the hydraulic gear to operate the locks when the keeper is not present.

*Powered operation*

On large modern canals, especially very large ones such as ship canals, the gates and paddles are too large to be hand operated, and are operated by hydraulic or electrical equipment. On the Caledonian Canal the lock gates were operated by man-powered capstans, one connected by chains to open the gate and another to draw it closed. By 1968 these had been replaced by hydraulic power acting through steel rams. Even on smaller canals, some gates and paddles are electrically operated, particularly if the lock is regularly staffed by professional lock keepers. On the River Thames below Oxford all the locks are staffed and powered. Powered locks are usually still filled by gravity, though some very large locks use pumps to speed things up.

*Fish ladders*

The construction of locks (or weirs and dams) on rivers obstructs the passage of fish. Some fish such as lampreys, trout and salmon go upstream to spawn. Measures such as a fish ladder are often taken to counteract this. Navigation locks have also potential to be operated as fishways to provide increased access for a range of biota.

*Weigh lock*

A weigh lock is a specialized canal lock designed to determine the weight of barges to assess toll payments based upon the weight and value of the cargo carried. The Erie Canal had weigh locks in Rochester, Syracuse, and West Troy New York. The Lehigh Canal also had weigh locks.

Picture 8.12 A weigh lock on the Lehigh canal

## Special cases

### *Lock flights*

Loosely, a flight of locks is simply a series of locks in close-enough proximity to be identified as a single group. For many reasons, a flight of locks is preferable to the same number of locks spread more widely: crews are put ashore and picked up once, rather than multiple times; transition involves a concentrated burst of effort, rather than a continually interrupted journey; a lock keeper may be stationed to help crews through the flight quickly; and where water is in short supply, a single pump can recycle water to the top of the whole flight. The need for a flight may be determined purely by the lie of the land, but it is possible to group locks purposely into flights by using cuttings or embankments to "postpone" the height change. Examples: Caen Hill locks, Devizes.

"Flight" is not synonymous with "Staircase" (see below). A set of locks is only a staircase if successive lock chambers share a gate (i.e. do not have separate top and bottom gates with a pound between them). Most flights are not staircases, because each chamber is a separate lock (with its own upper and lower gates), there is a navigable pound (however short) between each pair of locks, and the locks are operated in the conventional way.

Picture 8.13 The flight of 16 locks at Caen Hill on the Kennet and Avon Canal

However, some flights include (or consist entirely of) staircases. On the Grand Union (Leicester) Canal, the Watford flight consists of a four-chamber staircase and three separate locks; and the Foxton flight consists entirely of two adjacent 5-chamber staircases.

*Staircase locks*

Where a very steep gradient has to be climbed, a lock staircase is used. There are two types of staircases, "real" and "apparent".

A "real" staircase can be thought of as a "compressed" flight, where the intermediate pounds have disappeared, and the upper gate of one lock is also the lower gate of the one above it. However, it is incorrect to use the terms staircase and flight interchangeably: because of the absence of intermediate pounds, operating a staircase is very different from operating a flight. It can be more useful to think of a staircase as a single lock with intermediate levels (the top gate is a normal top gate, and the intermediate gates are all as tall as the bottom gate). As there is no intermediate pound, a chamber can only be filled by emptying the one above, or emptied by filling the one below: thus, the whole staircase has to be full of water (except for the bottom chamber) before a boat starts to ascend, or empty (except for the top chamber) before a boat starts to descend. By building a pair of such lock sets (one used to climb and the other to descend) these difficulties are avoided, as well as enabling a greater traffic volume and reduced wait times.

In an "apparent" staircase the chambers still have common gates, but the water does not pass directly from one chamber to the next, going instead via side ponds. This means it is not necessary to ensure that the flight is full or empty before starting.

Examples of famous "real" staircases in England are Bingley and Grindley Brook. Two-rise staircases are more common: Snakeholme Lock and Struncheon Hill Lock on the Driffield Navigation were converted to staircase locks after low water levels hindered navigation over the bottom cill at all but the higher tides – the new bottom chamber rises just far enough to get the boat over the original lock cill. In China, the recently completed Three Gorges Dam includes a double five-step staircase for large ships, and a ship lift for vessels of less than 3000 metric tons. Examples of "apparent" staircases are Foxton Locks and Watford Locks on the Leicester Branch of the Grand Union.

Operation of a staircase is more involved than a flight. Inexperienced boaters may find operating staircase locks difficult. The key worries (apart from simply being paralyzed with indecision) are either sending down more water than the lower chambers can cope with (flooding the towpath, or sending a wave along the canal) or completely emptying an intermediate chamber (although this shows that a staircase lock can be used as an emergency dry dock). To avoid these mishaps, it is usual to have the whole staircase empty before starting to descend, or full before starting to ascend, apart from the initial chamber.

Picture 8.14 Staircase of five locks, dating from 1774, at Bingley, England

One striking difference in using a staircase of either type (compared with a single lock, or a flight) is the best sequence for letting boats through. In a single lock (or a flight with room for boats to pass) boats should ideally alternate in direction. In a staircase, however, it is quicker for a boat to follow a previous one going in the same direction. Partly for this reason staircase locks such as Grindley Brook, Foxton, Watford and Bratch are supervised by lockkeepers, at least during the main cruising season, they normally try to alternate as many boats up, followed by down as there are chambers in the flight.

As with a flight, it is possible on a broad canal for more than one boat to be in a staircase at the same time, but managing this without waste of water requires expertise. On English canals, a staircase of more than two chambers is usually staffed: the lockkeepers at Bingley (looking after both the "5-rise" and the "3-rise") ensure that there are no untoward events and that boats are moved through as speedily and efficiently as possible. Such expertise permits miracles of boat balletic: boats travelling in opposite directions can pass each other halfway up the staircase by moving sideways around each other; or at peak times, one can have all the chambers full simultaneously with boats travelling in the same direction.

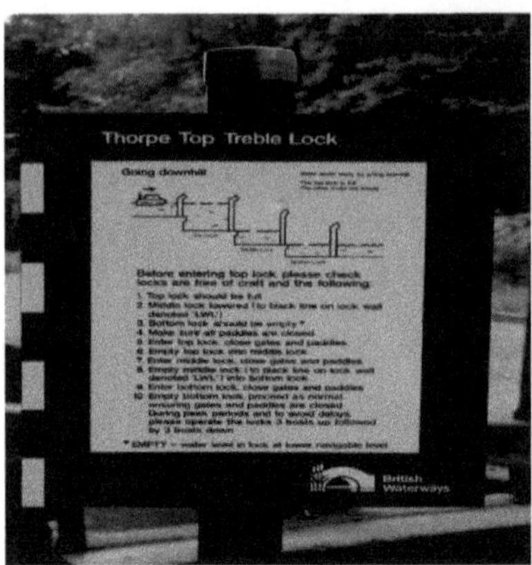


Picture 8.15 Instructions for descent of treble staircase, Chesterfield Canal

*Doubled, paired or twinned locks*

Locks can be built side by side on the same waterway. This is variously called doubling, pairing, or twinning. The Panama Canal has three sets of double locks. Doubling gives advantages in speed, avoiding hold-ups at busy times and increasing the chance of a boat finding a lock set in its favour. The Belgian Company SBE Engineering worked on this project. There can also be water savings: the locks may be of different sizes, so that a small boat does not need to empty a large lock; or each lock may be able to act as a side pond (water-saving basin) for the other. In this latter case, the word used is usually "twinned": here indicating the possibility of saving water by synchronizing the operation of the chambers so that some water from the emptying chamber helps to fill the other. This facility has long been withdrawn on the English canals, although the disused paddle gear can sometimes be seen, as at Hillmorton on the Oxford Canal. Elsewhere they are still in use; a pair of twinned locks has been opened in 2014 on the Dortmund-Ems Canal near Münster, Germany.

The once-famous staircase at Lockport, New York was also a doubled set of locks. Five twinned locks allowed east- and west-bound boats to climb or descend the 60 feet (18 m) Niagara Escarpment, a considerable engineering feat in the nineteenth century. While Lockport today has two large steel locks, half of the old twin stair acts as an emergency spillway and can still be seen, with the original lock gates having been restored in early 2016.

Picture 8.16 Doubled locks. Left lock has boat in it, right lock (center of drawing) is empty. This is on the Erie Canal at Lockport.

These terms can also (in different places or to different people) mean either a two-chamber staircase (e.g. Turner Wood Double Locks on the Chesterfield Canal: the same canal has a three-rise staircase called Thorpe Low Treble locks), or just a flight of two locks (as at Thornhill Double Locks on the Calder and Hebble Navigation). Also, "double lock" (less often, "twin lock") is often used by novices on the English canals to mean a wide (14 ft) lock, presumably because it is "double" the width of a narrow lock, and allows two narrow boats going in the same direction to "double up". These are properly known as broad locks.

*Stop locks*

A "stop" lock is a (very) low-rise lock built at the junction of two (rival) canals to prevent water from passing between them.

During the competitive years of the English waterways system, an established canal company would often refuse to allow a connection from a newer, adjacent one. This situation created the Worcester Bar in

Birmingham, where goods had to be transshipped between boats on rival canals only feet apart.

Where a junction was built, either because the older canal company saw an advantage in a connection, or where the new company managed to insert a mandatory connection into its Act of Parliament, then the old company would seek to protect (and even enhance) its water supply. Normally, they would specify that, at the junction, the newer canal must be at a higher level than their existing canal. Even though the drop from the newer to the older canal might only be a few inches, the difference in levels still required a lock – called a stop lock, because it was to stop water flowing continuously between the newer canal and the older, lower one. The lock would be under the control of the new company, and the gates would, of course, "point" uphill – towards the newer canal. This would protect the water supply of the newer canal, but would nevertheless "donate" a lockful of water to the older company every time a boat went through. In times of excess water, of course, the lock "bywash" would continuously supply water to the lower canal.

Picture 8.17 Lifford Lane guillotine lock, Kings Norton, Birmingham, between the Stratford-upon-Avon Canal and the Worcester and Birmingham Canal

When variable conditions meant that a higher water level in the new canal could not be guaranteed, then the older company would also build a stop lock (under its own control, with gates pointing towards its own canal) which could be closed when the new canal was low. This resulted in a sequential pair of locks, with gates pointing in opposite directions: one example was at Hall Green near Kidsgrove, where the southern terminus of the Macclesfield Canal joined the Hall Green Branch of the earlier Trent and Mersey Canal. The four gates stop lock near Kings Norton Junction, between the Stratford-upon-Avon Canal and the Worcester and Birmingham Canal was replaced in 1914 by a pair of guillotine lock gates which stopped the water flow regardless of which canal was higher. These gates have been permanently open since nationalization.

Many stop locks were removed or converted to a single gate after nationalization in 1948. Hall Green stop lock remains, but as a single lock: the extra lock was removed because the lowering of the T&M's summit pound (to improve Hare castle Tunnel's "air draught" – its free height above the water level) meant that the T&M would always be lower than the Macclesfield. The Hall Green Branch is now considered to be an extension of the Macclesfield Canal, which now meets the T&M at

Harding's Wood Junction (just short of the Hare castle Tunnel north portal).

The newer canal was not always at a higher level than the one it joined. For instance, there is a very shallow lock at Autherley Junction, where the 1835 Birmingham and Liverpool canal (now part of the Shropshire Union Canal) met the older Staffordshire and Worcestershire Canal, built in 1772. The Nicholson guide shows that a boater travelling south along the newer canal locks "up" before turning north or south onto the older Staffordshire and Worcestershire Canal – so the Shropshire Union Canal gains a small lockful of water each time a boat passes. However, the gain is tiny since the level difference is so small that it is sometimes possible to open both gates at once.

*Round locks*

There are several examples where locks have been built to a round plan, with more than two exits from the lock chamber, each serving a different water level. Thus, the lock serves both as a way of changing levels and as a junction. The circular plan of the lock allows boats within it to rotate to line up with the appropriate exit gate.

The best-known example of such a round lock is the Agde Round Lock on the Canal du Midi in France. This serves as a lock on the main line of the canal and allows access to the Hérault River.

Picture 8.18 Agde Round Lock

A second French round lock can be found in the form of the, now disused, Écluse des Lorraines, connecting the Canal latéral à la Loire with the River Allier.

*Drop locks*

A drop lock allows a short length of canal to be lowered temporarily while a boat passes under an obstruction such as a low bridge. During canal restoration, a drop lock may be used where it is impractical or prohibitively expensive to remove or raise a structure that was built after the canal was closed (and where re-routing the canal is not possible).

A drop lock can consist of two conventional lock chambers leading to a sump pound, or a single long chamber incorporating the sump – although the term properly applies only to the second case. As the pounds at either end of the structure are at the same height, the lock can only be emptied either by allowing water to run to waste from the sump to a lower stream or drain, or (less wastefully) by pumping water back up to the canal. Particularly in the two-chamber type, there would be a need for a bypass culvert, to allow water to move along the interrupted pound and so supply locks further down the canal. In the case of the single-chamber type, this can be achieved by keeping the lock full and leaving the gates open while not in use.

Picture 8.19 Dalmuir drop lock

While the concept has been suggested in a number of cases, the only example in the world of a drop lock that has actually been constructed is at Dalmuir on the Forth and Clyde Canal in Scotland. This lock, of the single chamber type, was incorporated during the restoration of the canal, to allow the replacement of a swing bridge (on a busy A road) by a fixed bridge, and so answer criticisms that the restoration of the canal would cause frequent interruptions of the heavy road traffic. It can be emptied by pumping – but as this uses a lot of electricity the method used when water supplies are adequate is to drain the lock to a nearby burn.

*Flood locks*

A flood lock is to prevent a river from flooding a connected waterway. It is typically installed where a canal leaves a river. At normal river levels, the lock gates are left open, and the height of the canal is allowed to rise and fall with the height of the river.

However, if the river floods beyond a safe limit for the canal, then the gates are closed (and an extra lock created) until the river drops again. Since this is a true lock, it is possible for boats to leave the canal for the flooded river despite the difference in water levels (though this is not likely to be wise) or (more sensibly) to allow boats caught out on the flood to gain refuge in the canal.

Note that if the canal is simply a navigation cut connecting two stretches of the same river, the flood lock will be at the upstream end of the cut (the downstream end will have a conventional lock).

Flood locks which have been used only as flood gates (see below) are often incapable of reverting to their former purpose without refurbishment. That is, where only outer gates are ever closed (probably because a waterway is not a true commercial one, and therefore there is no financial imperative for a boat to venture out onto a flooded river) inner gates soon suffer from lack of maintenance. A good example is on the Calder and Hebble Navigation, where structures referred to in the boating guides as "Flood Locks" are clearly only capable of being used for flood-prevention, not for "penning" boats to or from the river in flood.

### *Flood gates*

A flood gate or stop gate is the cheaper equivalent of a flood lock. Only one set of gates exist, and so when the river is higher than the canal, the gates are closed and navigation ceases. These are quite common in the French inland waterways system. Flood gates may also be used to sub-divide long canal pounds or protect, in case of bank collapse, the surrounding area if this is lower than the water level of the canal. They are commonly found at the ends of long embankments and at aqueducts. These gates are often overlooked because they lack balance beams and are only a little higher than normal canal level.

Picture 8.20 Flood gate or stop gate (American usage) on Chesapeake and Ohio Canal. When a flood threatened, boards were put in the lock to divert waters from the canal to the Potomac River. Note winch house on top for the boards.

### *Bi-directional gates and locks*

Where a lock is tidal (i.e. one side of the lock has water, whose level varies with the tide) or where a canal meets a river whose level may vary, the water on the tidal or river side (the "downstream" side) may rise above the water on the normal "upper" side. The "upstream" pointing doors will then fail to do their job, and will simply drift open. To prevent water flowing the wrong way through the lock, there will need to be at least one set of gates pointing in the "wrong" direction. If it is desirable that boats can use the lock in these circumstances, then there needs to be a full set of gates pointing towards the tidal or river side. The usual method is to have gates pointing in opposite directions at both ends of the chamber (alternatively, the "paired stop lock" arrangement of two separate sequential locks pointing in opposite directions would work here – but would require an extra chamber). If navigation is not required (or impossible) at one "extreme" (e.g. allow navigation above mid-tide, but just prevent the canal emptying at low tide) then it is only necessary to have one set of bi-directional gates.

Picture 8.21 (a) Bi-directional flood gates on the Dessel–Turnhout–Schoten Canal, Belgium (b) Bi-directional gates at one chamber end of a tidal lock (located in Veurne on the Nieuwpoort–Dunkirk Canal)

Picture 8.21 Two types of bidirectional locks at the end of the Marne–Rhine Canal in the Independent Port of Strasbourg

*Tidal locks*

A sea lock is one that connects a canal or river directly with an estuary or ocean. A tidal lock is generally any lock that connects tidal with non-tidal water. This includes a lock between a tidal river and the non-tidal reaches, or between a tidal river and a canal, or a sea lock. However, the term usually refers specifically to a lock whose method of operation is affected by the state of the tide. Examples:

- A canal joining a river whose levels are always lower than the canal. All that is needed is an ordinary lock, with the gates pointing up the canal. The lock is used normally so long as the tide is high enough to float boats through the lower gates. If near low tide the lock becomes unusable, then the gates can be barred (and simply become a "reverse flood gate", holding water in the canal). This arrangement also applies to some sea locks (e.g. Bude Canal).
- A canal joining a river which is normally below it, but which can rise above it (at very high tides, or after heavy rain). One pair of gates can be made bidirectional, i.e. the inward-pointing gates would be supplemented by a pair pointing out to the river. When the river is higher than the canal, the normal gates would just drift open, but the additional pair of gates can be closed to protect the canal, and prevent navigation to the river. In effect, we have simply added a flood gate.

Picture 8.22 Sea lock at Bude, Cornwall

- As above, but where it is safe to navigate even when the river is higher than the canal. The lock will be fully bidirectional (two pairs of oppositely pointing gates at each end) to allow boats to pass at any normal river levels. At extreme low or high tides unsuitable for navigation, the appropriate sets of gates are barred to prevent passage.

*Inlet locks*

An inlet lock is to regulate water from a feeder canal or a river into the main canal. In some cases, the inlet lock may double as a lift lock to allow boats into the river slack water. Note that in the example on the right, the feeder canal was originally George Washington's Little Falls Skirting Canal which was part of the Potomac Company's canals, later re-purposed as a feeder canal for the Chesapeake and Ohio Canal.

Picture 8.23 Inlet lock (left) from feeder canal, regulates water from the Potomac River into the C&O canal. Lift lock (right) allows boats to continue up the canal in a normal fashion.

*Very large locks*

The world's largest lock was, until 2016, the Berendrecht Lock, giving access to the Port of Antwerp in Belgium. In 2016 the Kieldrecht Lock in the same port became the largest. The lock is 500 m (1,600 ft) long, and 68 m (223 ft) wide and drops 17.8 m (58 ft), and has four sliding lock gates. The size of locks cannot be compared without considering the difference in water level that they are designed to operate under. For example, the Bollène lock on the River Rhône has a fall of at least 23 m (75 ft), the Leerstetten, Eckersmühlen and Hilpoltstein locks on the Rhine–Main–Danube Canal have a fall of 24.67 m (80.9 ft), each and the Oskemen Lock on the Irtysh River in Kazakhstan has a drop of 42 m (138 ft). The total volume of water to be considered in any lock equals the product of its length, breadth and the difference in water levels. Lock staircases are used in an attempt to reduce the total volume of water required in relation to the amount of useful work done. The useful work done relates to the weight of the vessel and the height it is lifted. When a vessel is lowered the consumption of potential energy of the water consumed is considered. An alternative to locks is a boat lift; facilities of this type, e.g. the Anderton boat lift or the Strépy-Thieu boat lift in Belgium, do not rely on the consumption of water as the primary power source, are powered by motors and are designed to consume a minimum amount of water.

Picture 8.24 (a) Berendrecht Lock (right) and Zandvliet Lock (left), located at the entrance to the Port of Antwerp (top) from the Scheldt (foreground) (b) Barges at a lock on the Mississippi River

The 29 locks on the Mississippi River are typically 600 feet (180 m) long while tug and barge combinations are as much as 1,200 feet (370 m) long consisting of as many as 15 barges and one tug. In these cases, some of the barges are locked through, using partially opened lock valves to create a current to pull the un-powered barges out of the lock where they are tied up to wait for the rest of the barges and the tug to pass through the lock. It can take as much as an hour and a half to pass the lock.

The gates of a Guillotine lock work in a way similar to a sluice gate, but most canal lock gates are hinged to swing like doors.

*Hiram M. Chittenden Locks*

Every November, the large lock of the Hiram M. Chittenden Locks (better known locally as the "Ballard Locks" in reference to the Seattle neighborhood they are located in) was emptied for maintenance, as seen in the November 2004 pictures below. This provides an opportunity to visualize how a lock works without the water obscuring the bottom of the lock. For reference, the picture far left shows the lock in operation, with a tug and a barge (loaded with sand and gravel) waiting for the gates to open. In the bottom left corner of the picture may be seen the cut-out in the side wall that contains the gate when open.

The lock has three pairs of gates, one pair at each end and one pair in the middle so that half the length of the lock can be used when the whole length is not required, thus saving water. The barely visible person walking along the bottom of the lock in the second picture gives an indication of the vast size of this lock. In both pictures of the end gates, the string of penstock opening is visible along the sides at the bottom. The water entering and leaving the lock flows by gravity through these openings. It requires around 15 minutes to fill or empty the lock.

Picture 8.25 Hiram M. Chittenden Locks: tug and barge in lock when full.

*Van gate*

This type of gate was a Dutch invention in the early 19th century. The Van gate has the special property that it can open in the direction of high water solely using water pressure. This gate type was primarily used to purposely flood certain regions, for instance in the case of the Hollandic Water Line. Nowadays this type of gate can still be found in a few places, for example in Gouda.

The design of a Van gate is shown in the image on the lower right. When the tube connecting the separate chamber with the high-water level side of the sluice is closed and the connection with the low water level side opened, the water level in the separate chamber will drop to the level on the low water level side of the sluice. The surface area of the gate separating the chamber from the high-water level side of the sluice is larger than that of the gate closing the sluice. This results into a net force that opens up the sluice.

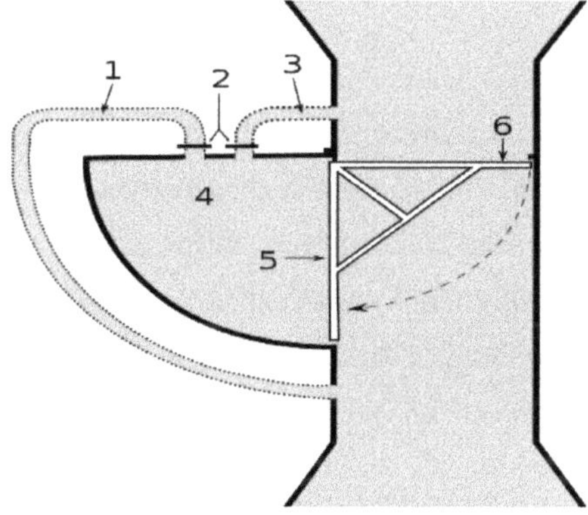


Picture 8.26 A Van Gate

1: Tube connecting the chamber to the high-water side of the sluice, 2: Gates to regulate the water level in the chamber, 3: Tube connecting the chamber to the low water side of the sluice, 4: The chamber in which the water level can be controlled, 5 Door with larger surface, 6: Door with smaller surface.

## History and development

*Dams and weirs*

In ancient times river transport was common, but rivers were often too shallow to carry anything but the smallest boats. Ancient people discovered that rivers could be made to carry larger boats by making dams to raise the water level. The water behind the dam deepened until it spilled over the top creating a weir. The water was then deep enough to carry larger boats. This dam building was repeated along the river, until there were "steps" of deep water.

*Flash locks*

The development of dams and weirs created the problem of how to get the boats between these "steps" of water. An early and crude way of doing this was by a flash lock. A flash lock consisted essentially of a small opening in the dam, which could be quickly opened and closed. On the Thames in England, this was closed with vertical posts (known as rymers) against which boards were placed to block the gap.

When the gap was opened, a torrent of water would spill out, carrying a "downstream" boat with it, or allowing an "upstream" boat to be man hauled or winched through against the flow. When the boat was through, the opening would be quickly closed again. The "gate" could also be opened to release a 'flash' downstream to enable grounded boats to get off shoals, hence the name.

This system was used extensively in Ancient China and in many other parts of the world. But this method was dangerous, and many boats were sunk by the torrent of water. Since this system necessarily involved lowering the level in the pound, it was not popular with millers who depended on a full head of water to operate their equipment. This led to constant battles, both legal and physical, between the navigation and milling interests, with rivers being closed to navigation if there was any shortage of water. It was mainly this conflict, which led to the adoption of the pound lock in medieval China, as this means that relatively little water is consumed by navigation.

*Staunch*

A more sophisticated device was the staunch or water gate, consisting of a gate (or pair of mitred gates) which could be closed and held shut by water pressure when the river was low, to float vessels over upstream shallows at times of low water. However, the whole upstream head of water had to be drained (by some auxiliary method approaching modern sluices) before a boat could pass. Accordingly, they were not used where the obstacle to be passed was a mill weir.

*Pound lock*

The natural extension of the staunch was to provide an upper gate (or pair of gates) to form an intermediate "pound" which was all that need be emptied when a boat passed through. This type of lock, called a pound lock was known in Imperial China and Europe.

Pound locks were first used in medieval China during the Song Dynasty (960–1279 AD). The Songshi or History of the Song Dynasty, volume 307, biography 66, records how Qiao Weiyue, a high-ranking tax administrator, was frustrated at the frequent losses incurred when his grain barges were wrecked on the West River near Huai'an in Jiangsu. The soldiers at one double slipway, he discovered, had plotted with bandits to wreck heavy imperial barges so that they could steal the spilled grain. In 984 Qiao installed a pair of sluice-gates two hundred and fifty feet apart, the entire structure roofed over like a building. By siting two staunch gates so close to one another, Qiao had created a short stretch of canal, effectively a pound-lock, filled from the canal above by raising individual wooden baulks in the top gate and emptied into the canal below by lowering baulks in the top gate and raising ones in the lower.

Picture 8.27 Model of early river pound lock, constructed in Lankheet water park, Netherlands

*Turf-sided lock*

A turf-sided lock is an early form of canal lock design that uses earth banks to form the lock chamber, subsequently attracting grasses and other vegetation, instead of the now more familiar and widespread brick, stone, or concrete block wall constructions. This early lock design was most often used on river navigations in the early 18th century before the advent of canals in Britain. The sides of the turf-lock are sloping so, when full, the lock is quite wide. Consequently, this type of lock needs more water to operate than vertical-sided brick- or stone-walled locks. On British canals and waterways most turf-sided locks have been subsequently rebuilt in brick or stone, and so only a few good examples survive, such as at Garston Lock, and Monkey Marsh Lock, on the Kennet and Avon Canal. Both these locks are in the canalized river section of the canal and so are over supplied with water.

Picture 8.28 The turf-sided Monkey Marsh Lock on the Kennet & Avon Canal at Thatcham

**Material:** The gates are made generally in pairs and are of,

(a) Wood, and

(b) Iron.

**Wooden gates:** They consist of a series of horizontal beams of green heart, (plain or framed) spaced closer towards the bottom to resist the water pressure, and joined together by a heel post and meeting post at the two extremities and uprights in the middle. Over the beams are fixed close sheeting of boards on the inner face (picture 8.29).

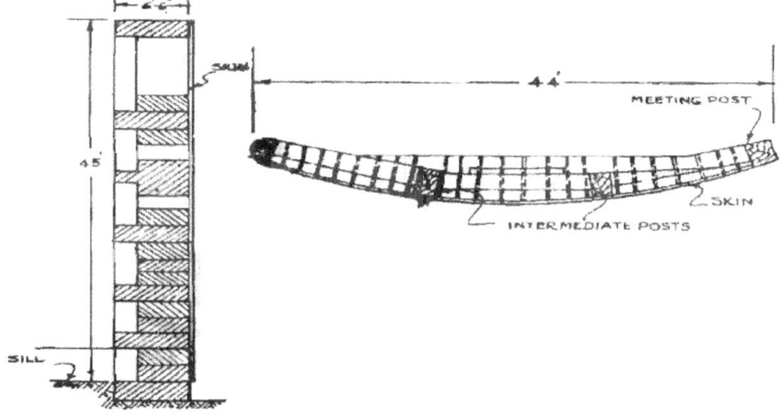


Picture 8.29 Wooden Lock Gates

**Iron gates:** Iron gates consist of plate iron ribs fixed horizontally and vertically and covered over with a skin of iron sheeting. The thickness of plate ribs are increased, and the spacing of the ribs reduced towards the bottom to withstand the increasing water pressure (picture 8.30).

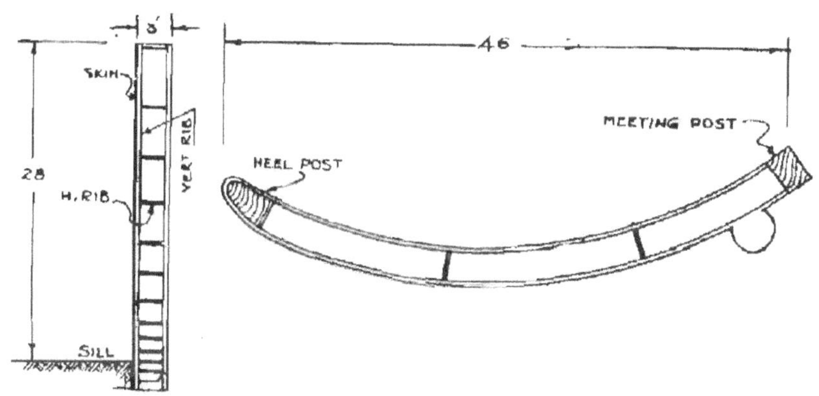


Picture 8.30 Lock Gates

**Forces on the gates:** The stresses that a gate has to bear are,

(1) A transverse stress due to the water pressure against the inner face that increasing with the depth of water;

(2) A compressive stress along the gate due to the pressure imposed by the other gate at the meeting, which is a component of the water pressure reaction. This compressive force is equal to the product of half the water pressure and the tangent of half the angle between the closed gates, as shown below: (picture 8.31)

Consider a pair of lock gates AB, AC, having a risen, the width of the lock being S. Let the length of each gate be equal to L.

Water pressure on AB = wL, if w is the unit pressure per foot length of gate, and acts at the middle point of AB.

The reaction at either end of AB = wL/2.

The reaction at the meeting post will be horizontal and in the direction AO.

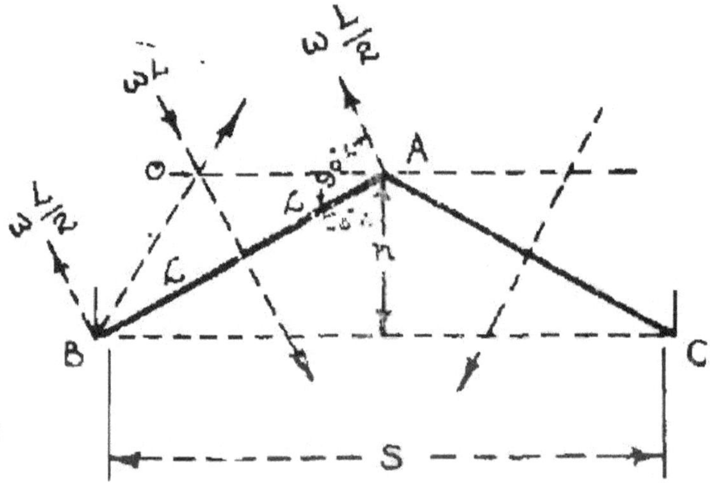


Picture 8.31

Therefore the reaction at the heel post must pass through O, the intersection of the other two forces.

Thus,

$\angle OAB = \angle OBA$, and

$\angle OBA = \angle ABC$

$\tan ABC = 2n/S$

The component of heel reaction along AB

= (wL/2) cotα

= (wL/2) (S/2n) (Product of half the water pressure n and tangent of half the angle between the gates).

=wLS/4n, which is the compressive force on the gate.

It could thus be seen that the compressive force varies inversely as the 'rise'. Thus, a large rise will decrease this stress, but by increasing the rise the length of the gate will be increased, which will increase the transverse stress due to water pressure on the gate. This will also increase the length of the lock. A good compromise is achieved by adopting a rise of 1/4 or 1/5·

**Shape of gates:** The shape of gates in plan has an important bearing on the strength of gates. Gates are usually straight or curved.

The straight gate is subjected to forces as discussed previously and have to be designed accordingly.

The curved gate is strong against the transverse water pressure, and on account of the arched shape, the transverse stress gets decreased as the curvature increases and the two gates together form a circular arch, when the transverse stress is completely changed to longitudinal compression. Thus, the stress becomes wholly compressive. This of course varies with the depth of the gate, as the section of the gate at the bottom gets the maximum compressive stress. These gates are theoretically the best type. But such gates have the following draw backs. i.e.,

(a) They are longer and costlier.

(b)They require large gate recesses.

(c)The gate sills will have to be curved, which is difficult and costly to construct. So, as a compromise, gates with a small curvature on the inside and with a straight sill are constructed (picture 8.2).

**Support for dock gates:** The gate is fitted with a pivot cap at the bottom of the heel post, which rests and revolves on a steel pivot embedded on the floor. At the top it is fixed by an encircling anchor strap, which is tied back to the wall. Where the gate is long and heavy it is provided with castors or, rollers, under the free end to ease the overhanging weight. These rollers are provided with roller paths on the gate floor (picture 8.32).

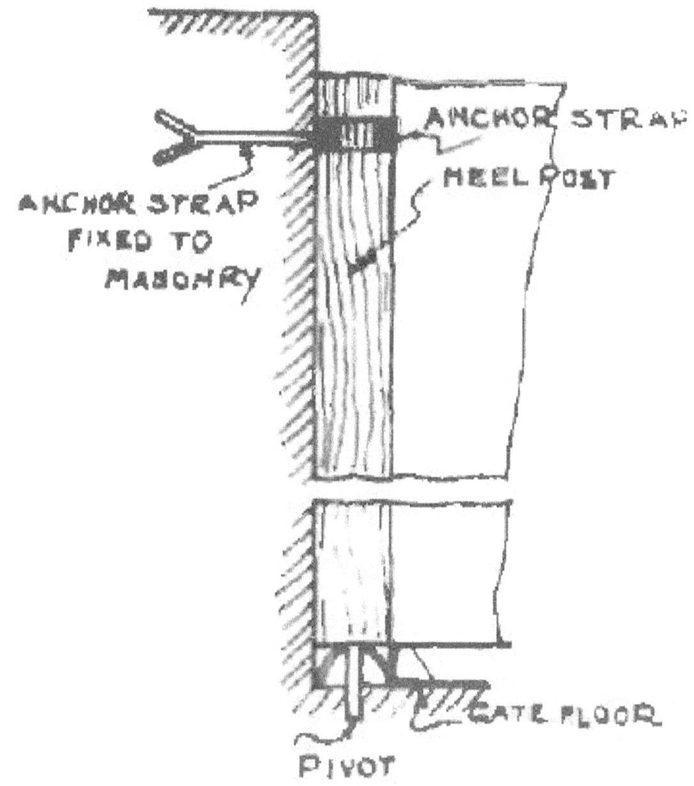


Picture 8.32 Heel Post of Gate

**Working of gates:** The gates are usually opened and closed, by two sets of chains, one for opening and the other for closing and operated simultaneously. These chains are fastened to each gate at one third its height on both sides, near the free end. Various mechanical devices have also been adopted for this purpose.

# 9. Quays

Platforms or landing places are necessary for ships to come close enough to the shore, for purposes of embarkation, disembarkation etc., at the same time. These platform locations should give sufficient depth of water for the ship to float. Such platforms are called Wharves. They are built out into or on to the water. Wharves along and parallel to the shore are generally called Quays and their protection walls are called quay walls (picture 9.1.)

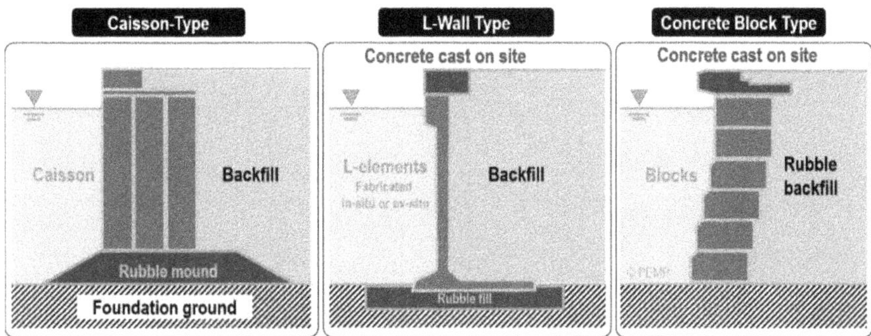


Picture 9.1 Quay walls types

Those that project into the ship's fairway or basin, at right angles or oblique from shore are known as Piers.

**Design of quay wall:** Quay walls are built to retain and protect the embankment or filling.

Factors affecting the design are:

(1) Character of foundation.

(2) Horizontal pressure to be provided for.

Quay walls are designed similar to retaining walls but on the water side they are subject to varying water pressure (owing to level variations due to tides), and on the land side, earth and containe water pressures, with proper allowances for surcharge.

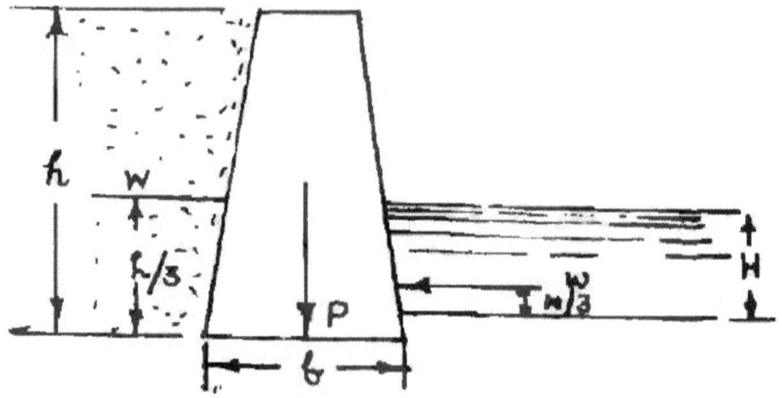


Picture 9.2 Forces acting on Quay wall

(1) *Horizontal pressure*: Generally, the contained water on the land side stands at a higher level especially at low tide. Hence a rapidly falling tide exposes the wall to a combined earth and water pressure from the land side. This is the most critical condition. Taking unit length of wall,

Water pressure = $\frac{w_1 h^2}{2}$

Earth pressure = $\frac{w_2 h^2}{2} tan^2 \left(45° - \frac{\Phi}{2}\right)$

Combined pressure = $\frac{h^2}{2}[w_1 + w_2 tan^2(45° - \frac{\Phi}{2})]$

Where, $w_1$ = weight of 1 c.ft of sea water,

$w_2$= weight of 1 c.ft of earth behind the wall,

$\Phi$ = angle of repose of the earth,

h = height of wall.

(2) *Overturning moment:* It is caused by the moment of differential head. Consider a unit length of wall.

Total equivalent liquid pressure (W) acts at a height $\frac{h}{3}$ on the shore side and water pressure (w) acts at a height $\frac{H}{3}$ on the waterside, at low level.

Taking moments about the base,

The differential moment = W * $\frac{h}{3}$ - $\frac{wH}{3}$ tending to overturn.

For equilibrium, this overturning moment has to be balanced by the weight of wall and the counter moment. Hence.

$$P * \frac{b}{2} = W * \frac{h}{3} - \frac{wH}{3}$$

**Construction of Quay Walls :** These walls have to be founded under water and constructed in water.

The various types of wall construction are as follows:

(i) *Solid wall types* are founded on wells, caissons and mounds, and raised above water by masonry construction or large concrete blocks (picture 9.3 and picture 9.4).

(ii) *Dwarf quay wall types* founded on piles are also built. (Piles should be immersed always under water, if of timber). These are economical for river ports and ports having very moderate traffic (picture 9.5)

(iii) Timber lattice work jetties carried on iron piles or cylinders provide the cheapest form of quays, during the initial stages of port development.

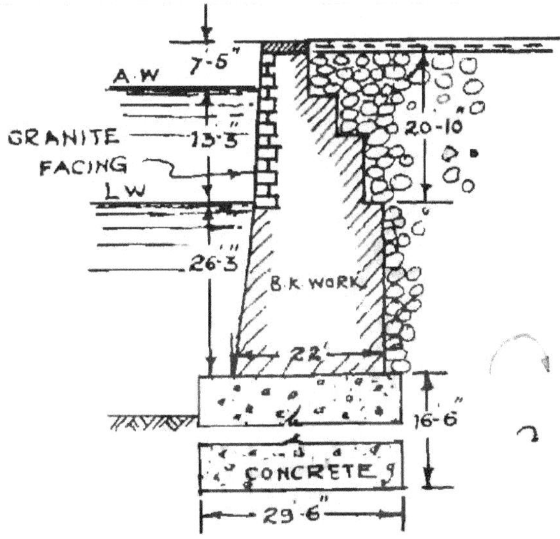


Picture 9.3 Solid Quay Wall

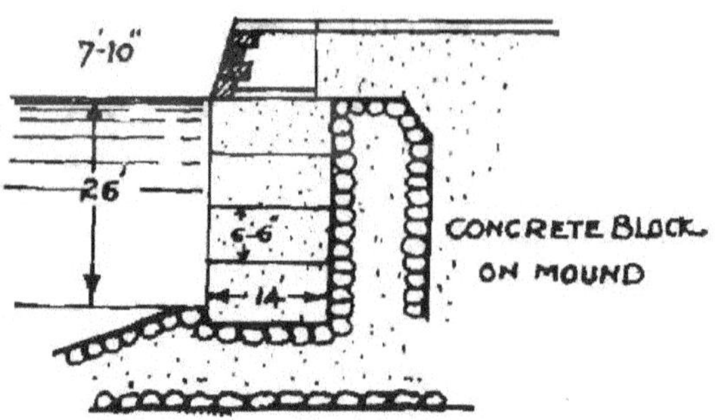


Picture 9.4 Solid Quay Wall

The driest and most durable materials should be put at the back of the quay walls, such as rubble, slag, granite to minimise pressure caused by back filling (picture 9.5).

Maritime quay walls must be extended into deep water for vessels of the largest displacement, such depths varying from 25' to 36'.

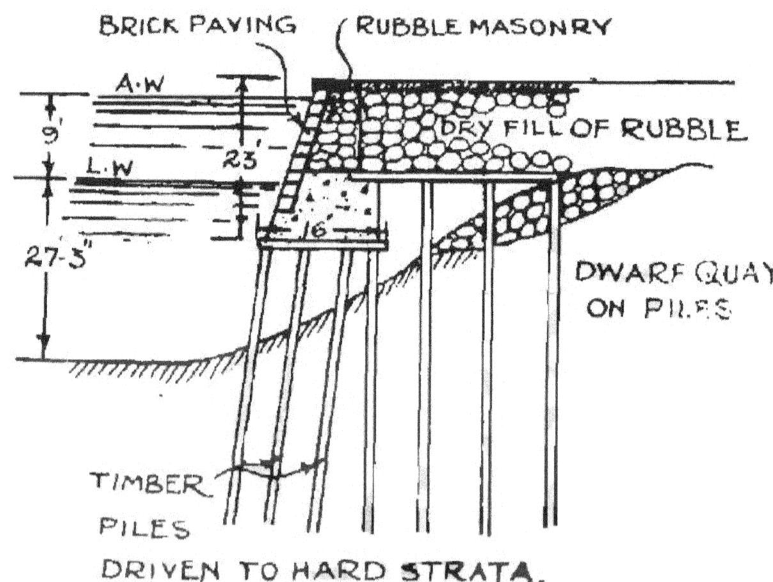


Picture 9.5 Quay walls on Pile

In long quay walls expansion joints at every 66' is necessary. These are designed to permit irregular movements of adjoining sections but to lock them to prevent horizontal break (picture 9.6).

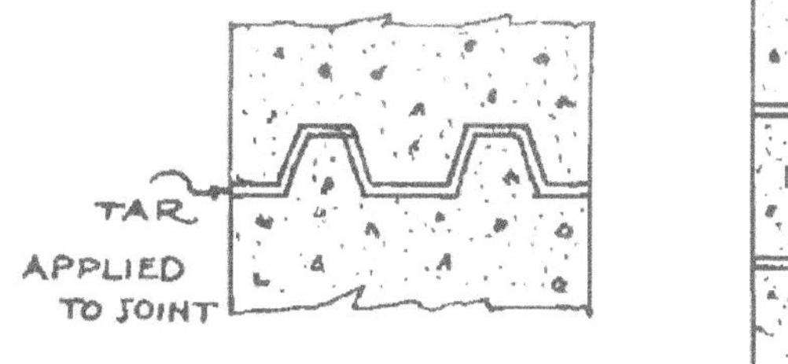


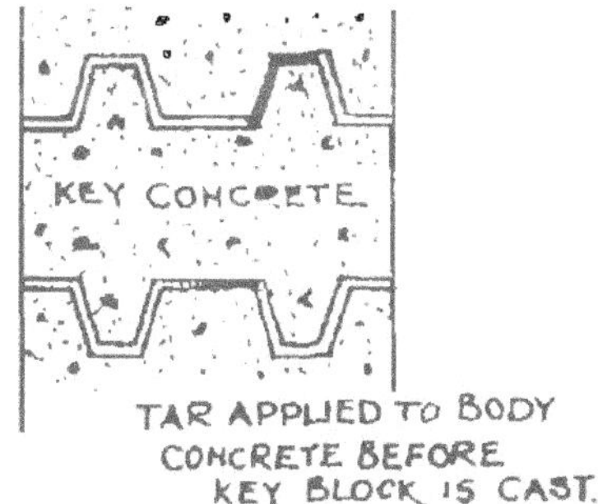


Picture 9.6 Expansion joints on Quay Walls

# 10. Transit Sheds and Ware houses

**Transit sheds:** These are the sheds of one or two storeys in height, the floor area being devoted to the handling and distribution of incoming and outgoing cargo requiring protection and used for storage of cargo for a short time. Hence these should be capable of affording flood space for storage of incoming cargo and accumulation of cargo ready for loading into the vessel (picture 10.1).

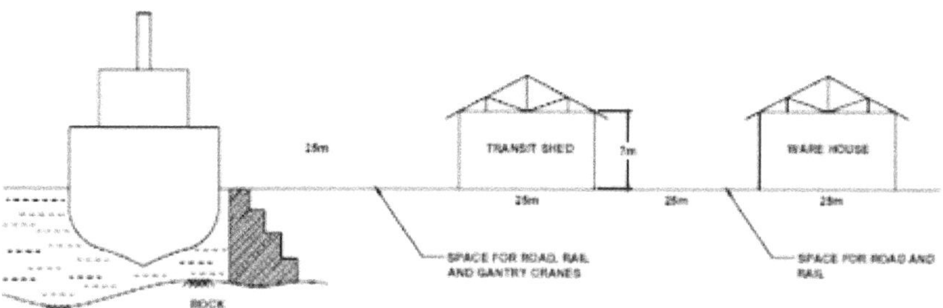


Picture 10.1 Transit shed

*Construction requirements:*

(1) Doors should be provided for ready and rapid opening and closing (folding or sliding doors could be employed).

(2) Construction should be light and fire resisting (as goods are only in transit and no need to store in safety for a long time).

(3) Should have ample lighting provided by long continued sky lights during day time and ample artificial lights for working at night time.

(4) Should have modern fire fighting apparatus.

*Other requirements:*

(1) Should be adjacent to the quay.

(2) Should have big capacity for storing incoming and outgoing cargo at the same time.

(3) Provision of road and rail for quick transit of cargo.

(4) Equipment like portable cranes for handling cargo should be adequate.

Picture 10.2 shows a typical transit shed constructed of steel and of large dimensions (width 180' inside).

Roadway runs through the shed; and railways lines run on the quay and behind the shed. The maximum capacities, floor area and quay space with respect to each running foot length of quay are the prime factors to be considered. For the shed shown in the figure we have per running foot length of quay,

| | |
|---|---|
| Capacity of shed | 5012 c. ft. |
| Floor area of shed | 19·9 sq. yd. |
| Quay space | 4·0 sq. yd. |

*Ware houses* are permanent structures, usually provided on shore or directly behind transit sheds for goods to be stored for a lengthy duration.

When such ware houses are for storing dutiable cargo remaining under customs authority, until cleared, they are called Bonded ware houses.

Modern ware houses are built of R.C.C. with many floors (see picture 10.3).

They include buildings, devoted to special purposes, such as grain storage, meat storage etc., special types of construction and equipment for each type of material will be required. Hence in the equipment, special storing bins and spouts to empty grains at floor levels refreigeration plants for cold storage etc., have to be put in. Loading and unloading arrangments, like light cranes may have to be put up at intermediate floor levels so as to reach top floors and bottom floors alike.

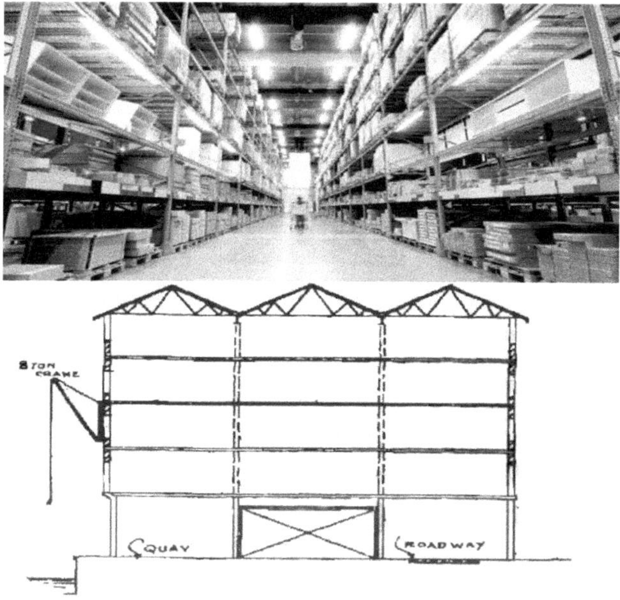


Picture 10.3 Warehouse

# 11. Maintenance Dredging

Dredging is the excavation of material from a water environment. Possible reasons for dredging include improving existing water features; reshaping land and water features to alter drainage, navigability, and commercial use; constructing dams, dikes, and other controls for streams and shorelines; and recovering valuable mineral deposits or marine life having commercial value. In all but a few situations the excavation is undertaken by a specialist floating plant, known as a dredger.

Dredging is carried out in many different locations and for many different purposes, but the main objectives are usually to recover material of value or use, or to create a greater depth of water. Dredges have been classified as suction or mechanical.

Dredging has significant environmental impacts: it can disturb marine sediments, leading to both short- and long-term water pollution, destroy important seabed ecosystems, and can release human-sourced toxins captured in the sediment.

**History**

Ancient authors refer to harbour dredging. The seven arms of the Nile were channelled and wharfs built at the time of the pyramids (4000 BC), there was extensive harbour building in the eastern Mediterranean from 1000 BC and the disturbed sediment layers gives evidence of dredging. At Marseille, dredging phases are recorded from the third century BC onwards, the most extensive during the first century AD. The remains of three dredging boats have been unearthed; they were abandoned at the bottom of the harbour during the first and second centuries AD.

During the renaissance Leonardo da Vinci drew a design for a drag dredger.

Dredging machines have been used during the construction of the Suez Canal from the late 1800s to present day expansions and maintenance. The completion of the Panama Canal in 1914, the most expensive U.S. engineering project at the time, relied extensively on dredging.

**Purposes**

- Capital dredging: dredging carried out to create a new harbour, berth or waterway, or to deepen existing facilities in order to allow larger ships access. Because capital works usually involve hard material or high-volume works, the work is usually done using a cutter suction dredge or large trailing suction hopper dredge; but for rock works, drilling and blasting along with mechanical excavation may be used.
- Land reclamation: dredging to mine sand, clay or rock from the seabed and using it to construct new land elsewhere. This is typically performed by a cutter-suction dredge or trailing suction hopper dredge. The material may also be used for flood or erosion control.
- Maintenance: dredging to deepen or maintain navigable waterways or channels which are threatened to become silted with the passage of time, due to sedimented sand and mud, possibly making them too shallow for navigation. This is often carried out with a trailing suction hopper dredge. Most dredging is for this purpose, and it may also be done to maintain the holding capacity of reservoirs or lakes.
- Harvesting materials: dredging sediment for elements like gold, diamonds or other valuable trace substances. Hobbyists examine their dredged matter to pick out items of potential value, similar to the hobby of metal detecting.
- Fishing dredging is a technique for catching certain species of edible clams and crabs. In Louisiana and other American states, with salt water estuaries that can sustain bottom oyster beds, oysters are raised and harvested. A heavy rectangular metal scoop is towed astern of a moving boat with a chain bridle attached to a cable. This drags along the bottom scooping up oysters. It is periodically winched aboard and the catch is sorted and bagged for shipment.

- Preparatory: dredging work and excavation for future bridges, piers or docks or wharves, this is often to build the foundations.
- Winning construction materials: dredging sand and gravels from offshore licensed areas for use in construction industry, principally for use in concrete. This very specialist industry is focused in NW Europe, it uses specialized trailing suction hopper dredgers self-discharging the dry cargo ashore. Land based old river beddings can be processed in this manner too.
- Contaminant remediation: to reclaim areas affected by chemical spills, storm water surges (with urban runoff), and other soil contaminations, including silt from sewage sludge and from decayed matter, like wilted plants. Disposal becomes a proportionally large factor in these operations.
- Flood prevention: dredging increases the channel depth and therefore increase a channel's capacity for carrying water.

**Other**

- Beach nourishment: this is mining sand offshore and placing on a beach to replace sand eroded by storms or wave action. This enhances the recreational and protective function of the beach, which are also eroded by human activity. This is typically performed by a cutter-suction dredge or trailing suction hopper dredge.
- Peat extraction: dredging poles or dredge hauls were used on the back of small boats to manually dredge the beds of peat-moor waterways. The extracted peat was used as a fuel. This tradition is now more or less obsolete. The tools are now significantly changed.
- Removing rubbish and debris: often done in combination with maintenance dredging, this process removes non-natural matter from the bottoms of rivers and canals and harbours. Law

enforcement agencies sometimes need to use a 'drag' to recover evidence or corpses from beneath the water.

- Anti-eutrophication: A kind of contaminant remediation, dredging is an expensive option for the remediation of eutrophied (or de-oxygenated) water bodies; one of the causes is like mentioned above, sewage sludge. However, as artificially elevated phosphorus levels in the sediment aggravate the eutrophication process, controlled sediment removal is occasionally the only option for the reclamation of still waters.
- Seabed mining: is a possible future use, recovering natural metal ore nodules from the sea's deepest troughs

**Disposal of the dredged material:** Dredged material is mainly disposed of in the following ways.

(i) Conveyed out to sea and deposited far from the site of accumulation.

(ii) Conveyed and deposited in swampy areas inland or adjacent to the shore for "reclamation" of land.

In respect of the above, state laws are established as to the disposal of the dredged material and have to be followed.

**Types of dredging devices:** The following are some of the modern types of mechanical dredges used in modern marine engineering practice.

(1) Dipper dredge.

(2) Grapple dredge.

(3) Continuous bucket or ladder dredge.

(4) Hydraulic or suction dredge:

A brief description of the working of these dredges is given in the below sections.

**Dipper dredge:** It consists of a floating vessel strongly constructed, carrying an inclined *'A frame* in the bow to hold the *boom B* by guy wires. Through the middle of the boom runs a dipper stick, worked by a rack and pinion arrangement and to the end of which is rigidly attached the dipper bucket *K*, with a flap. A hoist cable is fixed to the bucket, to move it up or down. The vessel is fixed to the bed in position by means of three stakes during the dredging operations. The boom *B* could swing horizontally, at the bow.

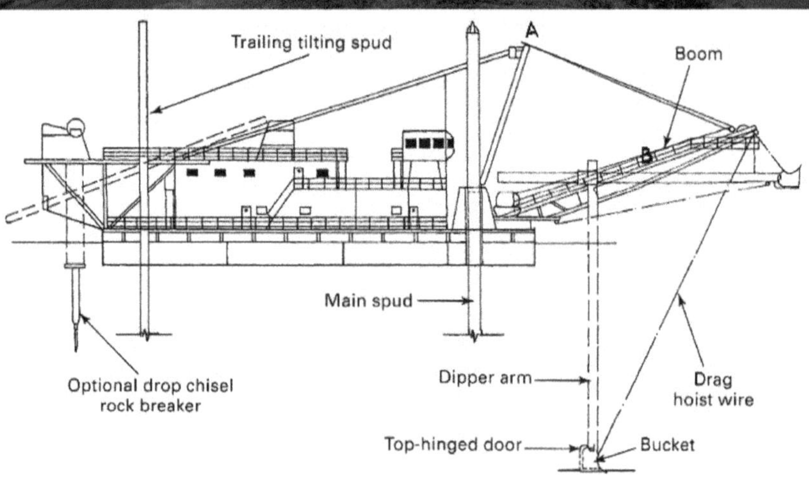


Picture 11.1 Dipper Dredge

**Operation:** The hoist cable is released, to enable the bucket to reach the bed when a crowding force is applied to the stick, through the rack and pinion forcing the teeth of the bucket to bite into the soil. The hoist cable is slowly pulled resulting in a cut being made in the bed. The hoisting is continued and the bucket is hauled out of the water, the boom *B* is swung round to deposit the material in the bucket, into any scow alongside or on to any predetermined place, by opening the flap. The boom is swung back, and the dipper lowered, in preparation for the next cut.

(1) Easy maneuverability and hence suitable for use in confined spaces around docks and narrow channels.

(2) Very powerful and capable of excavating in hard soil, for removal of boulders, and breaking up of heavy objects like old piles, cribs etc. This type of dredge, can dig in depths up to 50' of water and the dipper capacity varies from 1 to 5 c.yds. normally.

These types of dredges of heavy capacities of about 15 c.yds. were in use in the Panama Canal.

**Grapple dredge:** It consists of a substantial hull, to the front of which are fixed an 'A' frame and a boom *B*. The '*A*' frame is guyed back, by back legs. A grab bucket *K* is suspended by two cable lines H, H' called the opening and closing lines. The boom is fixed at the required elevation by means of a guy wire and arranged to rotate through a horizontal angle on a pivot at the lower end. The bucket hoisting lines pass over two main sheaves fixed to the upper end of the boom. The dredge is moored by the help of stakes fixed fore and aft.

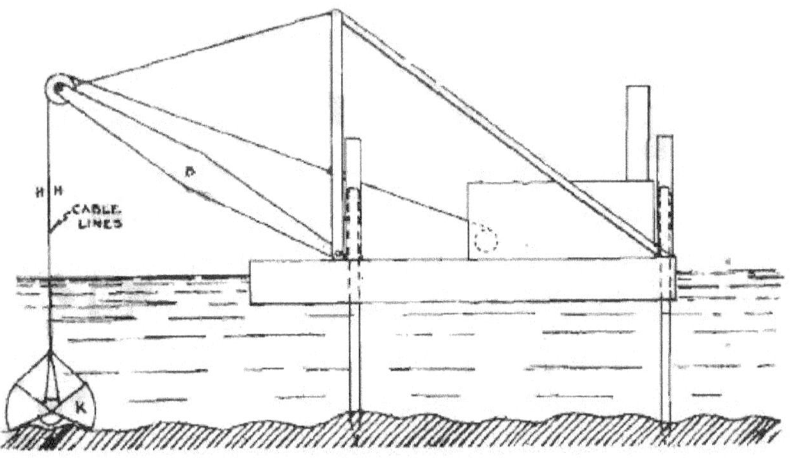


Picture 11.2 Grapple Dredge

**Operation:** After positioning the dredge, a scow is brought along side and tied fast to it, on the right side. The bucket is lowered to the bottom, where it bites the bed and fills itself. Then tension is put on the closing cable, which closes the bucket, hoists the load and swings the boom horizontally to the right. When the boom reaches over to the scow, the tension in the cables is reversed, and this results in the opening and discharging of the bucket and the boom swings back to the digging position as before.

The hull is generally 100 ft. to 200 ft. long and 50 ft. across, the booms being 50 ft. long. The capacity of the grab bucket ranges from 10 c.yds. up to 30 c.yds. This dredge is very efficient and suitable for dredging materials, like sand, clay or mud, but no good for hard diggings. The bed dredged by a grab will seldom be even and will exabit pits and high spots.

Continuous bucket Elevator or Ladder dredge: It consists of an endless chain of buckets, mounted and running round a ladder *L*, formed in the middle of the bow of a floating vessel. The ladder could be lowered or raised by the line *N*. The chain of buckets is operated, manually or mechanically by a big wheel *E*. The buckets are provided with pronged cutting edges.

**Operation:** Each bucket cuts and brings up material to the top of the ladder as the chain moves round, where each bucket inverts on descent and discharges its contents into special holds H.H. The vessel moves forward on completion of work at each section.

The size of these vessels is about 200 ft. in length and 50 ft. in width, having a draft of about 8 ft. to 10ft. These can be used for digging depths of 30 ft. to 40 ft. The average digging capacity of such a vessel is about 8000 c.yds. to 10000 c.yds. per day. This dredger is very suitable for handling coarse gravel or sand, hard clays and even soft or broken stone, at fairly good depths and beyond the reach of a dipper. The bed dredged is least disturbed.

Picture 11.3 Continuous bucket elevator or ladder dredge

**Hydraulic or suction dredge:** It consists of a suction pipe, carrying at the lower end a cutter of some sort and having a universal joint at top. This pipe is supported on a ladder and held in position by an *A* frame mounted on the bow of the dredging vessel. The suction pipe is connected to a centrifugal pump located amid ships having a long flexible delivery pipe discharging into hopper barges alongside the vessel itself or on to specially selected spot-on shore, needing reclaiming or filling.

**Operation:** The hull *V* carries the suction pipe 'S' on ladder, in the bow and the pumping machinery *P* is housed in the middle of the ship. with its delivery pipe *D* discharging into hopper barges floating behind the dredging vessel. The cutter is suspended from a frame in front and the vessel is moored by anchors. The cutter rotates, cuts and loosens the soil for quick and easy suction by the pump. The cut-up material is well churned in the operation, and mixed with water to facilitate suction.

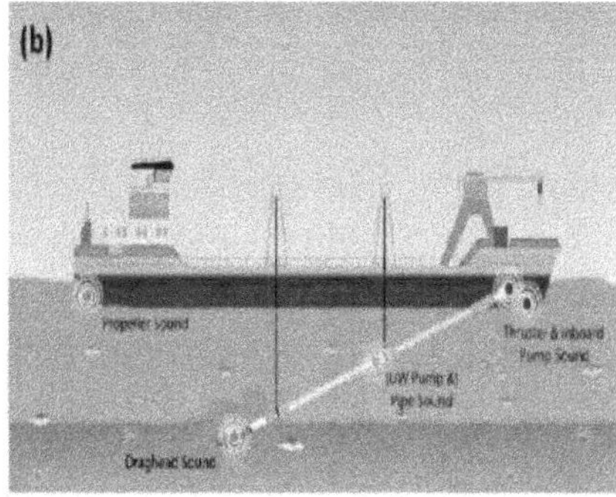

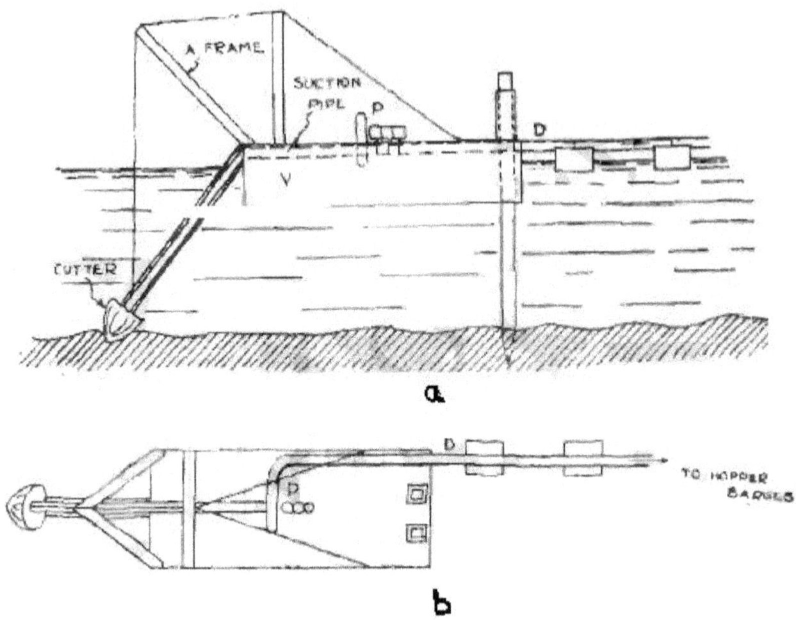


Picture 11.4 Haudraulic of Suction Dredge

Sea going dredges of this type have a size varying from 150 ft. to 450 ft. in length and 30 ft. to 50 ft. in width. The digging depths vary from 15 to 50 ft. The machinery is operated either by diesel power or electric power. The pump is a special type of centrifugal pump capable of handling heavy particles of dirt and rock brought out in dredging.

This type of dredge is very effective in beds of sand, silt, mud and clay in open water and is an excellent machine to clear sand bars. If big boulders or tree stumps are met with, they will have to be lifted out before putting the cutter to work. Gravel and soft rock are easily reduced by the cutter.

**Environmental impacts**

Dredging can create disturbance to aquatic ecosystems, often with adverse impacts. In addition, dredge spoils may contain toxic chemicals that may have an adverse effect on the disposal area; furthermore, the process of dredging often dislodges chemicals residing in benthic substrates and injects them into the water column.

The activity of dredging can create the following principal impacts to the environment:

- Release of toxic chemicals (including heavy metals and PCB) from bottom sediments into the water column.
- Collection of heavy metals lead left by fishing, bullets, 98% mercury reclaimed [natural occurring and left over from gold rush era].
- Short term increases in turbidity, which can affect aquatic species metabolism and interfere with spawning. Suction dredging activity is allowed only during non-spawning time frames set by fish and game (in-water work periods).
- Secondary impacts to marsh productivity from sedimentation.
- Tertiary impacts to avifauna which may prey upon contaminated aquatic organisms.
- Secondary impacts to aquatic and benthic organisms' metabolism and mortality
- Possible contamination of dredge spoils sites
- Changes to the topography by the creation of "spoil islands" from the accumulated spoil.
- Releases toxic compound Tributyltin, a popular biocide used in anti-fouling paint banned in 2008, back into the water.

The nature of dredging operations and possible environmental impacts cause the industry to be closely regulated and a requirement for comprehensive regional environmental impact assessments with continuous monitoring. The U.S. Clean Water Act requires that any discharge of dredged or fill materials into "waters of the United States," including wetlands, is forbidden unless authorized by a permit issued by the Army Corps of Engineers. As a result of the potential impacts to the environment, dredging is restricted to licensed areas only with vessel activity monitored closely using automatic GPS systems.

www.ingramcontent.com/pod-product-compliance
Lightning Source LLC
LaVergne TN
LVHW021154160826
845679LV00024B/2122

* 9 7 9 8 8 8 5 6 9 0 3 0 0 *